MIRACLE
IN ROOM 3123

ISBN: 978-1-947319-02-8

Cover and interior layout design: Kristi Yoder

Published by:
TGS International
P.O. Box 355, Berlin, Ohio 44610 USA
Phone: 330-893-4828
Fax: 330-893-2305
www.tgsinternational.com

TGS001531

MIRACLE
IN ROOM 3123

Bill & Pauline Miller
with Sherilyn Yoder

Dedication

Dedicated to God, "who forgiveth all thine iniquities; who healeth all thy diseases" (Psalm103:3).

and

To all the praying saints—"The effectual fervent prayer of a righteous man availeth much" (James 5:16).

Table of Contents

CHAPTER ONE

Christmas

The respirator hose dangled loosely from Bill's mouth. Pauline Miller stared at her husband, whose complete stillness added to her shock. Bill's eyes were closed, and his arms lay limp from sedation. The respirator was running at 100 percent, indicating that it could do no more to help Bill breathe.

Pauline glanced at her daughter, watching for her reaction. Judith, a registered nurse, would surely be able to make sense of it all. But Judith's eyes were wide with disbelief at the scene unfolding before them. Her knowledge of medicine helped her to understand the procedures, but it could not cure the helplessness she felt.

The medical team at Parkview Regional Medical Center in Fort Wayne, Indiana, hovered around Bill, inserting IVs, preparing medications, and discussing courses of action. Dr. Israbian, the specialist, detached himself from the group and approached Pauline.

"Mrs. Miller," he began, "your husband is very ill. Do you understand? He is deathly sick! We do not know if he will make it or not. He would have died if you hadn't brought him here. We do not know what is going on, but we are throwing everything at him that we think might help. He just isn't responding the way we would like."

Pauline listened with growing disbelief. Bill only had pneumonia! *Who dies from pneumonia?* she thought. *Not sixty-year-olds . . . right?* The weight of the pronouncement, the shock from the fast progression of events, and the fact that this was supposed to be a happy Christmas Day combined to form a squeezing pain in her heart. Her emotions built up and spilled out in tears.

Judith was crying too. "Mom," she said softly, "we have to make some phone calls."

Of course, Pauline thought. But how could they gather their wits enough to make sense on the phone? Still, she followed Judith out of the room and began to make a mental list of all the people who needed to be called.

"But Judith, it's Christmas morning!" she exclaimed. "If we call people from church and start the prayer chain, won't we spoil their day?"

Judith's breath caught on a sob. "They still need to know, Mom. And we need their prayers."

Mark and Norman were first on the list to be notified. Mark, the oldest of Bill and Pauline's three children, lived three hours east in Ohio with his wife Norma and five children. Norman, the youngest in the family, would have to make the trip with his wife Sharon and their four daughters from southern Ontario, where they were celebrating the holidays with Sharon's family. This meant they could make the trip in six hours instead of the usual sixteen from their home in northwestern Ontario.

Judith arranged for her husband, Tim, to bring their two sons to the hospital as soon as they could come. Even though they lived less than an hour away, Judith sensed a terrible urgency to have her family join her. A sudden question sprang to her mind: *Will this be our sons' last chance to see their grandpa?*

When they reentered Room 3123, Pauline and Judith were told Bill's blood pressure had dropped to 82/44. Nothing the medical staff did seemed to have any effect on the thick mucus filling Bill's lungs. After a nerve-jangling wait of several hours, Dr. Israbian approached Pauline again.

"Mrs. Miller, we have a narrow window of time in which to intervene. There is one more thing we would like to try, but we need your permission to do so. We have a machine called a RotoProne bed. The patient lies in the bed facedown while the bed slowly rotates from side to side. This therapy takes pressure off the lungs and helps with rest and recovery. It would be necessary to medicate your husband to paralyze him completely, keeping him from moving while in the bed. May we have your permission to do this?"

"Absolutely," Pauline replied without hesitation. "Please do whatever you can."

At 3:00 that afternoon, Mark Miller found his father strapped motionless inside something that looked like a space capsule. The enclosed bed moved slowly from side to side with Bill firmly secured inside. After repeating this motion for six hours, the bed would flip over completely to swing the patient on his back for one hour, and then resume its normal six-hour swing with the patient on his stomach.

Mark stared, shocked and incredulous. He could hardly see his father at all. One bare arm lay visible to onlookers, but the imprisoning metal machine covered up the rest of Bill's features. Mark touched the exposed arm hesitantly.

"Dad?" he said, nearly choking on the word. "This is Mark. I want you to work really hard on getting better." The arm didn't move.

A few hours later, Norman and Sharon arrived. Pauline met them on the first floor and escorted them to Room 3123. Inwardly she recoiled from entering the room again and seeing the still form of her husband, but she determined to do what had to be done. Norman walked around the machine, examining it from every angle.

"So many tubes," he murmured at last, noting everything hooked up to his father's body. After counting the many lines, Norman announced, "I think he has thirteen IVs!" He shook his head in disbelief. "It's hard to imagine what all they do."

At that moment, the bed began its first rotation, flipping Bill onto his back to change the pressure on his lungs.

"It's like a giant rotisserie," Norman observed wryly as the machine began its slow swing back and forth.

Weak smiles appeared on several faces at this comparison. Pauline, however, found it difficult to think of her husband roasting in a rotisserie. She shuddered involuntarily.

"Could we get out of here and go to the waiting room to talk?" she asked. Her family complied and followed her down to the waiting room. As they sat

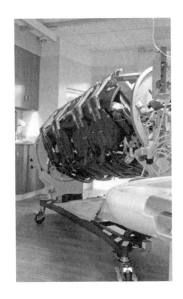

The RotoProne bed Bill was placed into on Christmas Day.

talking and catching up, two welcome faces appeared in the doorway. They were ministers from Bill and Pauline's church.

"The whole church has been praying since the prayer chain went around this morning," one of the men assured Pauline. "And we wanted to come and personally give you support and surround you with prayer."

Pauline closed her eyes with relief as the men prayed, allowing their petitions to lend comfort to her heart. The weakness and fear she felt nearly overwhelmed her, and the prayers were like an infusion of strength and peace directly into her soul.

At the end of visiting hours, the family checked on

Bill's oxygen saturation levels before they dispersed for the night. The oxygen levels had been dangerously low for several days, but it looked as though they were coming back up, however slowly. Could it possibly be safe to hope?

As Christmas Day, 2013, drew to a close, the in-laws took the children from the hospital to sleep at the homes of family members or friends. Mark, Judith, and Norman stayed at the hospital and slept as best they could in the waiting room. Pauline lay down on a couch in Bill's room, where sleep evaded her most of the night as she reflected on the whirlwind of recent events that had brought them to this place.

CHAPTER TWO

Downward Spiral

On December 17, Pauline had been putting on extra layers of clothing to ward off the encroaching chill when she heard coughing in the next room where her husband was dispatching his truck drivers over the phone.

"Bill!" she exclaimed. "That sounds awful. Are you going to be okay?"

Bill frowned. "I think so," he replied, "but maybe I'm getting bronchitis or something. Did I hear you say you have a doctor's appointment tomorrow?"

"Yes, I do have one at noon. Shall we check to see if the doctor can see you at the same time?" Pauline asked.

"I think that's a good idea," Bill said. "My chest feels really tight, and there's a lot of mucus in my throat. I really want to be over this thing before the children come home for our holiday family time."

The following day found Bill and Pauline being examined by their family doctor. After the doctor had listened to Bill's lungs, he remarked, "Well, your lungs sound clear, so it must be an upper respiratory problem. I'm going to prescribe an antibiotic that should clear up any infection. I also want you to take Mucinex to help loosen the phlegm, plus cough medicine as needed."

They did as they were told. Bill took all his medicines regularly and tried to rest more than usual. But instead of improving, his condition slowly worsened. Pauline began pulling out her arsenal of home remedies, concocting a drink here and rubbing on a poultice there. She set up the vaporizer to help her feverish husband's breathing. When Bill was awake, they discussed what could be going on with his body.

"Do you think it could be the adult form of RSV?"[1] Pauline wondered.

"Well, it's possible, since I was exposed to it when we took care of Bryce last week," Bill agreed. "But I didn't think it was usually serious for adults. This bug seems to be clamping down on me like a vise."

"You've been cooped up for several days now," Pauline noted. "Sometimes a body just needs a change of pace. Do you think you can come with me to Tim and Judith's house tomorrow? We're planning to do some Christmas baking, and I think it would do you good just to get out of the house and see your grandchildren."

"Whew . . ." Bill sighed wearily. "Just thinking about it makes me tired. Let me rest tonight, and then I'll see how I feel in the morning."

Saturday morning dawned, but Bill's coughing and

---

[1] Respiratory syncytial virus

weakness had not abated. In spite of that, he summoned enough energy to get into the car and go to Tim and Judith's house. Once he got there, he collapsed onto the couch and tried to smile at his grandchildren, Bryce and Trenton. Seeing that their normally enthusiastic grandpa was not able to play with them, they soon started their own game on the living room floor.

While Pauline and Judith whipped up gooey confections, Bill slept. He awoke to his daughter's voice saying, "Dad, we're getting ready for supper. Will you help us eat some pizza?"

Bill opened heavy eyelids. *Pizza?* His stomach turned at the thought. "Well, Judith . . ." he said slowly, "is there any chance you could make me some chicken noodle soup?"

Judith's eyebrows rose in surprise. "If that's what you'd like, Dad, I'll get it ready right away."

They sat down to supper, and Pauline noted her husband's flushed face. "Oh my, Bill," she said. "I don't think the day out did you much good after all. We'd better get you home soon."

At home, Bill's body temperature showed 102.3 degrees on the thermometer. "No wonder I feel like a tough piece of meat," Bill mumbled. Dosing up on a fever reducer, he went to sleep in the recliner. The next morning there was no question as to whether Bill should go to church or not. He lay in the recliner, coughs racking his frame every few minutes. "I really wanted to hear the baptismal applicants' testimonies today," he told Pauline weakly. "But I sure don't have any energy for that now." Those who were in the instruction class preparing to be baptized were scheduled to give their testimonies that day. It would be a special and deeply personal service.

"That's okay, Bill. You just rest, and I'll pick up a recording of the service for you," Pauline assured him.

When Pauline arrived home from church, however, Bill had no interest in listening to the CD she had gotten for him, or in eating lunch. He turned his face to the back of the couch. "I just want it quiet," he told his wife.

"Bill," Pauline coaxed, "can you get up for just a little bit and eat some soup? It'll give you strength." But even she was beginning to wonder whether anything could infuse strength into her ailing husband.

Bill ate tiny bites of soup and consented to listen to the recording of the service at Pauline's assertion that it would get his mind off being sick. But several hours later, after another painful coughing spell, he rasped to his wife, "I wonder if maybe I should go to the emergency room."

Pauline's eyes widened. "Are you really that sick, Bill?" she asked.

"Well, it'll be eighteen hours before I can get in to see the doctor again," Bill replied logically. What Pauline didn't know was that before she had gotten back from church, Bill had received a phone call from a friend who said numerous people in the area were coming down with pneumonia. The friend had urged Bill not to wait too long to get checked for it.

That phone call turned out to be a word from the Lord, as it encouraged Bill to admit he needed help promptly. Pauline drove Bill to the ER, where his oxygen saturation levels came in at 86, well below the normal range of 95–100. It didn't take long for the physician to order an X-ray of Bill's lungs. As soon as he had seen the X-rays, the doctor told Bill, "Mr. Miller, you have pneumonia in both lungs. I want you to immediately pursue treatment."

Bill guessed the implications. "You'd like to admit me, right? I'm ready to stay if that is what it takes." And so it was that he found himself settling into a room on the second floor of Parkview LaGrange Hospital. He lay meekly in bed as the nurses inserted IVs. Soon a dose of the usual medication for pneumonia dripped into his veins. Oxygen flowed into his nose and mouth, helping him to breathe. His oxygen saturation levels had continued to drop, now measuring only 83.

Pauline spent a restless night at the hospital. When Monday morning came, she could tell that Bill had been thinking about his business, which needed attention. "Pauline, why don't you go home and do the invoicing?" he asked her.

Pauline usually helped in the office two full days a week, plus a few extra hours here and there. They had started Lil' Digger Transport twenty-three years before as a means of hauling steel and other products with semi trucks. Over the years, it had grown to accommodate eleven trucks. Bill was kept busy dispatching loads, which consisted of telling the drivers where to go and coordinating their routes. He also waded through steady streams of administrative paperwork.

Concentrating would be hard, Pauline knew. Yet, the work needed to be done, and it might help get her mind off the fruitless worrying. She gathered a few belongings and headed home to Millersburg, a twenty-five-minute drive. Their office was attached to the house, which seemed suddenly too large for one lonely person. Pauline pecked away at the computer, each press of the keyboard echoing too loudly in the stillness. Her mind wandered. After a few hours, she decided it might be better to finish the invoicing the following day. She only wanted to be at her husband's side; it just didn't seem right to continue in her solitary labors while Bill languished in the hospital.

Pauline found Bill getting plenty of attention from the medical team, who monitored him diligently and tried to make him as comfortable as possible. A few visitors came, bringing snacks and support. Pauline was especially glad when Judith stopped in to check on her father. At the sight of the oxygen monitor, Judith's brows furrowed. "5L? That's really high." The "L" stood for liters, which was a measurement of the amount of oxygen flow. Oxygen was normally set between 2L and 3L.

Night fell, and Pauline decided it would be best to spend the night at home. That way she could finish her invoicing first thing in the morning and then head back to the hospital. Bill had appointed one of his former truck drivers to go ahead with the dispatching. Pauline was relieved that this detail had been arranged; the eleven drivers could go on with their jobs.

Concentration was still hard to come by on Tuesday morning. As Pauline tried to keep her mind on her work, Bill called from the hospital. "I think I feel a little better," he told her. "I took a shower and feel a bit stronger. Maybe I can get out of here in a day or two."

That was good news, but Pauline wondered if Bill was just trying to reassure her. She made a concerted effort to concentrate on her work for a few more hours before deciding it simply wasn't worth trying anymore. At noon, she traversed the nineteen miles back to the hospital to be with Bill.

"Well, the X-rays don't show any improvement," Bill told Pauline when she arrived in his room. Pauline looked at the X-rays, noting the cloudy white areas that told of suffocating gunk filling Bill's lungs.

"It sure is a stubborn case," Pauline replied, shaking her head. "Still, it's being treated well, and you should be getting better soon."

That afternoon, Bill got encouraging phone calls from both of his sons. Norman and Sharon had already started their holiday travel. They were spending some time in southern Ontario with Sharon's parents before heading down to Indiana.

As nightfall began spreading its blanket of darkness across northern Indiana on Christmas Eve, Bill's coughing increased. His breathing became labored, and his oxygen saturation levels declined even further. The oxygen meter was turned to 7L, and then to 9L.

"Bill," Pauline ventured, "what would you think about being anointed with oil?"

"I'd like that," Bill panted. "But when you call the bishop . . . just tell him to come when . . . it's convenient for him . . . since it's Christmas Eve."

"Sure," Pauline agreed. "It doesn't have to be done this evening."

Bill managed to eat a few bites of his supper, but nearly fell asleep during the meal. His whole body sagged with fatigue.

Tim and Judith were having family time with their sons when Pauline called to update them. "Do you want me to come?" Judith asked.

"I don't know, honestly," Pauline said wearily. "I don't think you have to. It's Christmas Eve, so you should probably just keep spending time with your family."

As the evening wore on, Bill's oxygen saturation levels continued to decline while the flow of oxygen through his meter continued to increase. The nurses now stayed in his room, no longer leaving between rounds of checking in. By 10 p.m., the oxygen flow was at its maximum of 15L. Bill's fingernails and lips had taken on a bluish cast. Her stress level rising, Pauline called Judith again and told her the oxygen saturation level was now at 77. Judith's reaction shocked her.

"Mom!" Judith cried out. "If it goes down to 75, it can be fatal!"

At this news, Pauline felt her whole body start to quiver. "Oh, please come, Judith!" she implored. "I can't make any more decisions by myself." Judith said she would be on her way shortly.

Pauline turned to the nurses. "Do you think it might be time to transfer Bill to a hospital in Fort Wayne?" she wondered.

"We're not sure, but we'll try the BiPAP machine on him here first," a respiratory therapist replied. "That may help to stabilize his breathing."

BiPAP stood for Bilevel Positive Airway Pressure. This machine was similar to a CPAP machine, which was commonly used for people with sleep apnea. It provided a constant stream of air to the patient's airways. A mask was placed over Bill's nose and mouth, and the machine began providing him with pressurized air.

Judith arrived at 11:00 that night. After assessing the situation, she told her mother it looked as though the BiPAP was doing its job. Bill's oxygen levels were slowly rising, and he seemed to be resting better. Around midnight, Judith left to go back home while Pauline tried to get some sleep.

A few hours later, Pauline padded back into her husband's room. He was shifting uncomfortably. And what was that bulge around his stomach area? She hurried over and touched the odd mound lifting the hospital gown and gasped in surprise. Bill's stomach was horribly bloated!

"Bill! Is that machine pumping air into your stomach?" she asked breathlessly. Without delay, she called a nurse, who confirmed that somehow the BiPAP machine was bypassing Bill's lungs and filling his abdomen with air. The machine was immediately removed, but Pauline sensed the nurse's question: *If we can't use the BiPAP, how will this patient get the oxygen he so desperately needs?*

Suddenly Pauline remembered a comment Judith had made about the oxygen machine during her visit. "I wonder why they don't have a full-face mask on him instead of just the nasal cannula?" Judith had remarked. So now Pauline decided to suggest the full-face mask to the nurse. With it, the oxygen might be able to more completely fill the nasal passages.

Her request was granted, and for the next several hours Bill remained somewhat stable, although immensely uncomfortable. Shortly after 6 a.m. on Christmas morning, he was visited by Dr. Kashyap.

"How do you feel, Mr. Miller?" the doctor asked.

"Fine," Bill replied. Pauline's heart skipped a beat. She hadn't expected her husband to evade the truth about such a weighty matter.

Dr. Kashyap knew there was more to Bill's statement as well. "No, Mr. Miller, tell me how you *really* feel," he insisted calmly.

"I feel fine," Bill repeated. "Oh, it hurts a little bit when I cough, but that's all."

Dr. Kashyap scrutinized his patient wordlessly for a few moments and then continued to question him in much the same vein as before.

Finally Pauline could take it no longer. "Doctor, he is *not* feeling fine! He has coughed so hard and breathed so hard for so long that he is getting used to it! He doesn't even realize how bad his condition is."

Dr. Kashyap gave her a slight nod and an understanding look. "Well," he said, "we can move him to the intensive care room and hook him up to the monitors so that the specialists in Fort Wayne can monitor him remotely. I will give him a double dose of another antibiotic to try to get rid of this bug. We will give it until 2 p.m. to see how he is by then. If there's still no improvement, we'll consider transferring him to Fort Wayne, if you're willing to do that. It is a costly transfer, but if it's necessary, we'll do it."

Bill looked at Pauline and nodded his assent. Pauline groaned within herself. *Bill needs help now*, she thought, *not this afternoon*. Still, she decided it would be best to follow the doctor's suggestion.

Just then Bill moved his arm a little, and almost immediately his oxygen levels decreased. Dr. Kashyap took in the details with a discerning eye and continued to talk with Bill while observing him closely.

Nearly half an hour later, the doctor seemed to reach a decision. He left the room, telling Pauline he was going to call the specialists at Fort Wayne. Five minutes later he was back. No longer just in observation mode, he began barking orders.

"Mr. Miller, you are being transferred to Parkview North in Fort Wayne right now. Yes, you will go in the ambulance with lights and sirens. You need to get on the respirator immediately to rest your lungs for a few days so your pneumonia can get better. You are already admitted to Room 3123. The only question is if we will intubate you here or take the chance and wait till you get there. The ambulance crew is prepared to stop beside the road and intubate on the way if they must. Do you understand? They will put you to sleep to put in the respirator."

The unexpected turn of events rattled Pauline's emotions again. Although tears ran down her cheeks, relief washed over her at the thought of Bill being under the care of more specifically trained doctors and more advanced medical equipment. But she needed to do some quick planning. After a hurried phone conversation with Judith, they decided Pauline should go home and have their neighbors take her on to the Fort Wayne hospital. Judith would drive directly down to Fort Wayne and meet the ambulance there.

Pauline knew she would have to hurry to see her husband before they intubated him at Fort Wayne. She scrambled to gather their belongings and headed home to Millersburg, nineteen miles southwest of Parkview LaGrange. While driving, she called Bill's sister Geneva to let her know about Bill's condition. Geneva could notify the rest of the siblings.

Shortly after she got home and gathered a few necessary items, Pauline was back in the car with their neighbors, Floyd and Ruth, speeding southeast toward Fort Wayne as fast as the snowy roads would allow. They were a little more than halfway to the hospital when Judith called again. "Mom, Dad is ready to be intubated. He wants to tell you something."

Pauline's heart sank. "Can't they wait to intubate until we get there?"

"No," Judith replied flatly. "The doctor's not waiting on anyone!"

When Judith gave the phone to her father, Pauline heard his husky, "I love you," before he was overtaken by a spasm of coughing so hard he couldn't hear her reply.

Oh, Lord, Pauline prayed desperately in her heart, *I'm not ready to live without this man. He's the one I've spent so much of my life with. We've raised a family together, moved here and there, worked at our business together . . . and I still need him so much! Please let him live.*

CHAPTER THREE

Life Together

Bill and Pauline had met in the church's youth group. Several Amish-Mennonite churches in northern Indiana joined up to form a youth group, and their numerous activities included volleyball, singing in nursing homes, socials, and work projects. After a social one evening, Bill decided to ask sixteen-year-old Pauline if he could take her home. This sort of escort was a customary casual date for those in the youth group, and Pauline consented to her young suitor's query. They had a nice chat that evening and decided they would like to see more of each other.

After a few casual dates, Bill asked Pauline if she would like to "go steady" with him. That meant they would date only each other while pursuing the possibility of marriage. Pauline agreed with a smile, and over the next six months they got to know each other well. Pauline enjoyed Bill's quick wit, strong leadership, and good values. His sisters were her good friends, so that was an added bonus. Bill loved how easy it was to talk with Pauline. When she smiled at him, his world brightened. He admired her family's stability, and he respected her father's sincerity and well-timed advice. In October of 1971, they got engaged and began planning for a June wedding.

Planning a wedding proved to be more stressful than they had anticipated. One detail nearly cost them their relationship. As Pauline was shopping for her guest servers' fabric, she settled on a popular style of the day. It was a lightweight fabric called White Rain, and it made soft, rustling sounds as it was being handled. Pauline thought the pale blue fabric was lovely. She had not expected her fiancé's opinion to differ, but differ it did. When Bill saw the fabric, it struck him as too thin and too noisy. It would draw too much attention, and he thought it simply wouldn't do. His reaction surprised and shocked Pauline, and she felt he was being unreasonable. After a serious disagreement, they began to wonder if they really were compatible enough to get married.

Finally Bill reached a dreaded decision. "I think we're going to have to call it off, Pauline," he said, his voice full of disappointment.

Pauline was upset enough to agree. During the next several hours, she began laying aside her wedding plans one by one. But as her hopes drained steadily away, she grew more and more unhappy. A pile of dreams, even her whole future, would crumble if Bill wasn't in them!

Neither of them slept well the night after their breakup. The decision simply didn't feel right, so eventually Bill picked up the phone and called Pauline. "Can we talk again?" he entreated.

They got together and prayed about their relationship and the disagreement. As they did so, God poured His grace on them and helped them to see how they could submit to each other and work through their disagreements. With renewed peace in their hearts and love for each other, they decided to keep their wedding date after all. After choosing a more suitable fabric for their helpers to wear, Bill and Pauline continued their wedding plans with less stress than before and with complete confidence that they were made for each other.

June 17, 1972, saw twenty-year-old Bill Miller and eighteen-year-old Pauline Graber get married on a perfectly beautiful day. Their love was joyful and built on a strong foundation of acknowledging God in all their ways. That foundation would see them through myriad shaky situations in the years to come.

The month after they were married, Pauline needed knee surgery. Two months later they lost their first child through miscarriage. At the time of their first anniversary, Pauline was just finishing the first trimester of her second pregnancy. The following month, however, she went into labor at four and a half months gestation. She delivered a fifteen-ounce girl whom they named Ruth Ann, but the tiny child lived only an hour.

Several months later, Pauline was expecting again and began hoping once more for a full-term pregnancy and a healthy baby. But it was not to be; she carried this child for five and a half months and delivered another girl. Martha Susan weighed less than two pounds and lived for only two hours.

The doctors diagnosed Pauline with a rare condition that caused her not to be able to carry a child once it had reached a certain weight. They finally decided it would be best to do corrective surgery, which meant the only option for delivery would be Caesarean section. Bill and Pauline were ready to take any steps that would enable her to have a healthy pregnancy, and they agreed to have the surgery done.

In March of 1975, Bill and Pauline decided to move to Kentucky and join an Amish-Mennonite community there. In December of that year, they were ecstatic to finally receive a healthy addition to their family, a boy named Mark Edward.

Less than a year later, the little family with a ten-month-old baby grew to include another member, a little girl named Judith Marie. Bill and Pauline rejoiced in the Lord's blessing and mercy even as they scrambled to pack two diaper bags and prepare two sets of bottles.

Life together held its challenges, but it was good.

CHAPTER FOUR

Walking with the Shadow

L ittle Mark was nearing his third birthday, and like many little boys, he loved to be with his daddy wherever he was. "I want to go to the bine-com," he told his mother one day, using his toddler word for "combine." So saying, he set off across the lane toward the big piece of farm equipment. Nobody foresaw the danger of the pickup truck that was just starting up. Mark's uncle started driving out the lane just as his nephew was toddling across it.

A terrifying *thump* sounded under the tires, and soon everyone was running to the scene. The pickup truck had not run over Mark, but it had knocked him over forcefully. Blood oozed out of his ears, and one eye was bloody.

The twenty-two-mile drive to the hospital seemed ever so long as Bill and Pauline tried to comfort their son. Pauline prayed desperately, "Lord, you know how much we wanted this child! Please don't take him from us now!"

Mark was diagnosed with facial cuts and internal bleeding, and he had to be in surgery for some time. But God graciously spared him, and he came through the surgery all right. How grateful his parents felt during his period of recovery! The shadow of death had come close, but God had not allowed it to touch their son.

A year and a half after Mark's brush with death, Norman Eugene was born into the Miller family. Bill and Pauline fell in love with him quickly, as did his brother and sister.

The years passed swiftly, and soon it was time to send Mark to school. Pauline helped with carpooling, sometimes taking several other children along in her car. One winter day, the steep hill between their home and the school was covered with ice. Pauline carefully made it up the hill and started slowly down the other side. Suddenly she saw a car near the bottom of the hill, partially blocking the road. In a panic, she hit the brakes, and her car spun around on the ice. Pauline's eyes widened as she looked fearfully at the deep hollow toward which she was headed. And then, miraculously, her front wheels touched the grass, stopping the car. She let out the breath she had been holding, at the same time breathing a grateful prayer to the God who had been watching over her and the schoolchildren.

In May of 1984, the phone rang with shocking news. An explosion had occurred in the basement of Pauline's parents' new home, causing a fire. Pauline's father had been seriously injured, with burns over 35 percent of his body, and lungs damaged by the LP gas. He needed to be on a respirator for more than two weeks, and his life was in danger even longer than that. Pauline greatly desired to help her mother and siblings, so she traveled to Indiana and stayed there for a week at a time, giving relief to those who were constantly taking care of her father. Bill would bring the children up on the weekends and then bring Pauline back home. The situation was not ideal, but circumstances were desperate, and Pauline felt the Lord's merciful hand sustaining her. She had the sense that God was bigger than the crisis they were facing and that He would take care of her and her family.

Busy, happy days followed until August of 1987, when they decided to move back to Indiana. Bill had found work on a chicken farm, along with a feed mill business. One of their family goals was to have chores for the children, and the new occupation seemed to be the answer to that goal.

A few years later the feed mill was sold, and the Miller family found themselves moving to a rental property in Middlebury, Indiana. Bill converted the feed truck into a semi and started hauling PVC pipe for a local business. Through this experience, he discovered that he enjoyed trucking, and eventually he named the trucking business Lil' Digger Transport.

The business ended up doing well for them and enabled them to buy an old house near Millersburg, Indiana, in 1991. They felt it was a blessing straight from God, but it certainly needed a lot of work to make it comfortable and livable. By this time Mark had finished school, and he ended up becoming the chief handyman, remodeling much of the house himself.

As the company grew and their children got older, Pauline became more involved with the business, working alongside her husband in their home office. Meanwhile, their children had growing dreams for occupations of their own.

Mark became proficient in operating an excavator, and he loved his work. He installed septic systems and dug basements with ease. Bill sometimes stood back and watched his precise work with amazement, commenting to his son, "You could tie a shoelace with that excavator!"

Judith dreamed of becoming a nurse, but it remained a distant goal while she found fulfillment in teaching school for several years. Then she assisted with midwifery at a local birthing center for nearly a year before traveling to Hillcrest Home to work with the senior residents there. After a term of voluntary service at Hillcrest, she was able to take nurses' training in conjunction with her work. After graduating, she found employment as a nurse in the emergency room at Parkview Fort Wayne, which she greatly enjoyed.

Norman, meanwhile, had an ongoing interest in flying airplanes. Bill asked him on his sixteenth birthday if he would rather have a car or flight lessons. "Flight lessons, of course," was his quick reply. Over the next four years he completed his training and began to work at the Warsaw airport, eventually obtaining his mechanic's license and instrument rating, which was required for a pilot to fly under instrument flight rules.

In April of 1994, God called Pauline's father home.

His burn injury had caused him to develop congestive heart failure over the years, which led to a heart attack. The sudden end to her father's life was hard for Pauline to work through. She missed him greatly as a father of whom she had many memories, while Bill missed the wise counsel and friendship he had found in his father-in-law.

Life continued with its series of ups and downs. Seeing their children get married ushered in a happy season for Bill and Pauline. In 1997, Mark got married to a former pen pal of his, Norma Lebold from Millbank, Ontario. Their reason for writing each other as young children was that they had discovered they were twins.

Another young lady, also from Millbank, boarded with the Millers during her tenure of teaching school with Judith. Sharon Kuepfer became like a second daughter and sister in the household. Norman became interested in solidifying their connection with Sharon, and they got married in 2002.

Four years later Norman and Sharon felt God calling them to serve on the mission field in Dryden, Ontario. Norman could use his piloting skills as a bush pilot in Canada, while at the same time working with Northern Youth Programs, a camp that provided spiritual direction for First Nations families.

After Norman and Sharon's commissioning service at church, refreshments were served. Judith found herself sitting across the table from a pharmacist named Tim Haines. They struck up a conversation and discovered their mutual medical interests. A spark of friendship was ignited, so Bill and Pauline invited Tim to eat with them at a restaurant to get to know him better. As they were enjoying their meal, an acquaintance of Tim's spotted him and came over to say hello. "What's this all about?" he asked curiously, eyeing their party.

With a twinkle in his eye, Tim replied, "It's all about mergers and acquisitions."

Indeed, the "merger" went through, and Tim and Judith were married in August of 2007. On the morning of the wedding, Judith made a trip to the cemetery and placed yellow roses on the graves of the two sisters whom she had never known. She remembered that if they had lived, they would have been her bridesmaids that day.

Sadly, the nightmare of the loss of an infant visited Tim and Judith as well. Their first child, a daughter named Kiersten, was born full-term and weighed over nine pounds. However, Judith experienced a complete placental abruption, and the emergency C-section was not performed in time to save the baby.

By this time Bill and Pauline were no longer strangers to walking with death, although it never got easier to face that shadow yet again. In 1998, Pauline's brother David died after fighting debilitating multiple sclerosis for twenty years. At the age of forty-five, he seemed too young to be leaving his wife and four children behind.

Bill's mother passed away unexpectedly from an aneurysm in 1999.

In 2004, Pauline's sister Susan was laid to rest after a battle with bone cancer. Only forty-nine years old, she left behind a husband and six children.

"Lord, what are you telling us through all these sad deaths?" Bill and Pauline asked. Eventually they found peace in placing their trust in a sovereign God who was creating an eternal, real heaven for all these people who had died in faith. Although their questions were not all answered, they grew in faith and belief in God's goodness and love.

Pauline's mother came to live with them in 2009. They enjoyed taking care of her for nine months until she suddenly became ill. In the hospital, the doctors diagnosed her with a heart attack and double pneumonia. In just a few days she received her eternal reward. Pauline imagined her mother being able to meet the precious souls of her other family members who were already living in the presence of Jesus, and the thought gave her a measure of peace.

Then in August of 2010, Bill's father was found dead in bed one morning. He had suffered from Alzheimer's for a few years, but his sudden death still came as a shock. Now Bill and Pauline were left without any parents, and they felt a bit lost. They realized they were now the older generation, responsible for passing everything important on to their children and grandchildren.

Relating to their grandchildren became a joyful occupation for Bill and Pauline. Mark and Norma gave them their first grandchild, Yvonne. At the time, Mark's family lived just across the yard. After frequent visits to their grand-daughter, Pauline was thrilled to observe that Yvonne recognized her. With every new grandchild, Bill and Pauline reveled in the connection they felt to each one.

. . . .

A unique ministry opportunity developed for Bill and Pauline after Ed Yoder, an Amish-Mennonite pastor serving in Ireland, came to their church for a series of meetings. They invited Ed over for a meal, and during their conversation, Ed told them about some people from Germany who had visited his church in Ireland. They were hungry for solid Biblical teaching and were interested in the Mennonite way of life. What they really needed was someone who spoke their native language to teach them from their German Bible and encourage them in a counter-cultural and often lonely way of life.

That was how Bill and Pauline met Heiko and Sabine Klein. The German couple had been on a long spiritual journey. When Sabine was growing up, she had a Mennonite pen pal from Georgia for several years, but they had since lost track of each other. Sabine imbibed the secular culture around her and eventually put God far from her mind. Heiko was of much the same persuasion, but God kept pursuing them through numerous events that they found hard to ignore.

One day as Heiko and Sabine were traveling together in

Italy, they came across a large rock with a sign mounted on it. Curious, they stopped to read it. "This is the place where the Hutterites met to worship in secret during the Reformation," it said.

Something clicked in Sabine's mind, connecting the Hutterites with her long-lost Mennonite pen pal. "Heiko," she said suddenly, "I need to get reconnected with the Mennonites. I think they have something I need." Thus, a spiritual odyssey began that would eventually lead them to attend a Mennonite family conference in Ireland, where they talked with Ed Yoder about what they longed for.

Bill and Pauline consented to meet with Heiko and Sabine in Germany, and they formed a lasting friendship. The teaching opportunities in Germany grew, and after several years, Bill and Pauline began making regular trips to that country to teach in various churches. They found fulfillment in the ministry God had given them.

. . . .

In the summer of 2013, Bill and Pauline made a trip to Ontario to visit their son Norman and his family. They lived at a family camp called Northern Youth Programs, and they had recently undertaken the enormous job of putting in a new septic system for the whole camp. Since they were now ready to spread topsoil, Bill willingly pitched in to help. He enjoyed running the bulldozer and spent five days spreading the soil. The Canada visit was a lovely time of doing useful work and getting to know their granddaughters better.

During the next few months, Bill noticed that he felt increasingly tired. He attributed it to getting older and attempted to continue his normal activities. In October, Bill and Pauline visited their son Mark and his family in Ohio. Mark had a roof repair job and invited his dad to help out, which Bill was happy to do. When Mark asked his dad to get a ladder out of the van, however, he was in for a surprise. Bill didn't have the strength to lift the twenty-eight-pound ladder out of the van! This was clearly unusual, even for a man who was "getting older." Bill was only sixty-one years old.

Later that month, Bill and Pauline left for Germany to visit Heiko and Sabine. The Kleins lived in a typical German home with steep steps leading to the upper floors. Climbing to the third-floor guest bedroom proved to be a tough task for Bill. He would stop at each landing to rest for a minute and catch his breath. Sabine noticed how hard her guest was breathing, and she became alarmed. "Bill, are you okay?" she asked.

"Yes, I'm just getting old," was Bill's cheerful reply.

They returned from Germany on November 4, and soon the weather began turning colder. That month Bill had a checkup with his doctor, and he told the physician about his fatigue as well as a sleep apnea problem. His heart checked out fine, and everything else seemed normal as well. The doctor scheduled a sleep test for Bill, and following that, Bill took a machine home to help with his sleep apnea.

Then cold weather really began to set in. Bill continued to feel run down, but he and Pauline were looking forward to the usual holiday festivities such as caroling, and especially to a cozy time of having their whole family together for the holidays.

And then the debilitating cough had begun.

CHAPTER FIVE

Day After Christmas

Bill lay in the RotoProne bed all night while Pauline tried without much success to get some sleep. Dawn came at last, and with it the welcome reassurance that Bill had survived the night. The doctor came in to talk with Pauline and her children. "Mrs. Miller," he said gravely, "your husband is still very ill. Rest assured that we are trying to do all we can!"

Yes, Pauline thought, *but there is Someone who can do more than that. I just wish I were able to rest and trust more fully in Him! Where is God right now?* In a flash, the answer came to her from Psalm 107, verse 6: "Then they cried unto the Lord in their trouble, and he delivered them out of their distresses." He was listening. He was present.

The doctor was telling them all he knew about Bill's condition. "When we intubated him, we swabbed for a culture and are still waiting for the results. They should be back shortly. For now, we've ruled out influenza and bacterial pneumonia. It could be viral pneumonia or an autoimmune disorder in which the body attacks itself, but we just don't know yet. If nothing shows up, we'll consider doing a lung biopsy to see if we can determine what is going on in there."

After the doctor left, Pauline and the children held a discussion about what needed to be done. Pauline told them about the verse God had reminded her of. Norman nodded in agreement. "But when will my heart catch up with what my mind knows?" he asked. "I know in my mind that God is here and that He cares, but letting that take care of my fear is really hard."

One of the things they needed to do was to get better sleep. They reserved two rooms at a nearby hotel for that purpose. One would be primarily for Pauline, and the other would be for family or whoever was staying with her. They were relieved to find out that the hotel offered discounts to families with loved ones in the hospital.

The events of the day became a blur. Bill's oxygen levels stayed about the same, but his blood gasses dropped. It seemed every time they turned around, there was something new to be concerned about. On each visit to Bill's room, they had to put on masks and gloves. When they left the room, they had to rub their hands with waterless antibacterial cream. Since only three people could be in his room at a time, they decided to allow only ministers and immediate family to go in and see him. They didn't want to become overwhelmed with visitors, especially with not knowing whether Bill's illness was contagious or not.

And visitors did come. They were respectful, compassionate,

and helpful. Sometimes they brought food. Other times they simply provided companionship and emotional support. In the afternoon of December 26, Bill's sister Becky and her husband Eddie Plank arrived from Georgia. It meant a lot to have family members travel so far to be with Bill and Pauline in their time of need.

As Pauline was processing their situation, one question stood out with alarming urgency: what would happen to their business? The possibility that Bill would never wake up loomed large in front of her, and she thought, *What if I never have a chance to ask him any more questions about how to run our business? I can't take all this responsibility!* The possibility overwhelmed her with heaviness.

That evening a minister from their church came to pay a visit along with his wife and daughter. They asked Pauline if they could pray for anything specifically, and Pauline shared her overwhelming worries about the business. As they prayed from their hearts, Pauline felt her burden lifting. Nothing had changed in her immediate circumstances, but she no longer felt the crushing heaviness she had before. Peace settled over her soul.

CHAPTER SIX

Marathon of Endurance

That night, Pauline slept at the hotel and was able to rest much better than she had at the hospital, although she still woke up very early on December 27. She had to see how her husband had fared during the night. His condition had not changed much, but they had a different doctor on duty that morning. He gave them no new information about Bill's condition, although he did say they had decided Bill was not strong enough for a lung biopsy. With that means of diagnosis no longer available, they would need to do more research to find out what was in his lungs.

Part of the research involved a family conference. That afternoon, Pauline and the children got together and talked with the doctor about the larger picture of Bill's life. What had his life been like, especially in the last several months? Stories started spilling out—conversations, anecdotes, travels. What stood out most in everyone's mind was the increasing fatigue that Bill had simply attributed to getting older. They talked about Germany and wondered if he could possibly have picked up a foreign germ there. Pauline mentioned that they had been in Dryden, Ontario, but that was back in June. His skin color had been poor during the last month, and he had gained fifteen pounds in the last year. Yet his EKG in November had shown nothing abnormal, so it seemed unlikely that his heart was in poor condition.

They talked and asked questions, but no answers seemed to be forthcoming. Pauline and her children left the room with troubled thoughts and desperate prayers. Judith said vehemently, "I just wish I knew what it was so I could get mad at it!"

Anger was only one of the emotions that came to the surface during these stressful moments. Some of the family members felt only a perplexity of questions, a vague hope, and a dull acceptance of reality. "After all," Mark said, "Dad will live one way or another, even if he doesn't live much longer in this life." Reminded of her belief in eternity and the faith that Bill would be with Jesus if he died, Pauline felt a slight measure of relief.

That evening they decided to have an anointing, as Bill had requested earlier. Calling the children, their spouses, and the ministers together, they met at 6:00. At that time the bed would go into the supine position so Bill would be faceup. That way they could better anoint his forehead with oil.

At the appointed time, two of the ministers gloved up and entered the room with Pauline and the children, while the third one stayed in the waiting room and held a short service for those gathered there.

In Bill's room, the bishop read James 5:13–16:

> Is any among you afflicted? let him pray. Is any
> merry? let him sing psalms. Is any sick among
> you? let him call for the elders of the church;
> and let them pray over him, anointing him with
> oil in the name of the Lord: and the prayer
> of faith shall save the sick, and the Lord shall
> raise him up; and if he have committed sins,
> they shall be forgiven him. Confess your faults
> one to another, and pray one for another, that
> ye may be healed. The effectual fervent prayer
> of a righteous man availeth much.

Then, placing a drop of oil on his gloved finger, he reached into the small opening in the rotating bed. Gently he rubbed the oil onto Bill's forehead just above his nose, the only place where his face was exposed. Another minister began praying, entrusting Bill into his Father's care. Everyone in the room felt the sacredness of the moment.

Dear Bill, can you hear us? Pauline whispered to him in her thoughts. She also hoped the doctors and nurses would be able to feel God's presence and know His power. *May this whole situation make your name more glorious, Lord,* she prayed.

Earlier that afternoon, another one of Bill's siblings had arrived. Geneva Chupp and her husband, Junior, had driven up from Kentucky. They cried and prayed at Bill's bedside, unable to comprehend how sick he really was. But their presence was another blessing to Pauline, strengthening her emotions.

It was decided that Mark would take Pauline home for the night, while several other relatives would stay at the hotel. As Mark and Pauline drove home, they discussed Mark's memory of several of his father's wishes, should anything ever happen to him. One thing Bill had done was to ask Glen Yoder, a former driver, to take care of the dispatching if he was unable to do it someday. Glen had consented and even now was helping to keep the company running.

One of Mark's friends called him as they were driving home. After hearing an update on Bill, the friend prayed over the phone for Mark and Pauline specifically. Pauline pondered this blessing and thought of the number of people who were praying even then for her husband. Emails were going out to relatives. Numerous churches were praying. Friends from Germany were being notified. From California to Germany, from the North to the South, people were raising heartfelt prayers for Bill's health. Pauline felt humbled and overwhelmed with gratitude. She would never be able to repay everyone's kindness!

When they finally arrived home, Pauline was struck by the sight of Bill's shoes on the floor beside his chair. *Will he ever put his feet into those shoes again?* The thought flashed unbidden through her mind. She saw his Bible on the stand beside the recliner. "Mark," she said suddenly, pointing, "please don't move those things. Leave them exactly where they are." Those tangible reminders of Bill seemed sacred at that moment.

Pauline crawled into bed, weariness enveloping her. *Lord,* she prayed silently, *please give me rest. Help me to be assured that even if I never feel Bill's warmth in this bed again, you will be my companion.* Her mind kept counting all the widows she knew. *Will that soon be my title as well?* She shook off the thought.

. . . .

Saturday, December 28, began at 3:30 a.m. for Pauline. Since no more sleep seemed to be in the forecast, she decided it would be a good idea to do some invoicing. She worked quietly so as not to disturb Mark and his family, who were occupying the basement. By 6:00, however, Mark was up and asked if he could help her. His assistance sped up the process of copying and mailing invoices. By 10:00 they were ready to head back to the hospital.

Bill's condition had not changed much through the night. His oxygen saturation levels had stabilized, and it seemed he was tolerating the rotating motion of the bed a bit better. They had experimented with turning him faceup every three hours instead of every six hours, and he had done all right with that. Yet these things were not necessarily definite signs of improvement. X-rays still showed his lungs to be almost full of phlegm. The PEEP settings on his ventilator were always set at unusually high levels. PEEP stood for "positive end-expiratory pressure," the amount of pressure it took to force oxygen into the lungs. Since his lungs were so congested, it took a lot of pressure to get enough air into them. At one point, Bill's PEEP setting was at 21, alarmingly close to the highest safe setting of 22.

The antibiotics had run their course. Bill had been on three different antibiotics, but none of them had proven effective. The doctors were now exploring other possible but unusual causes of pneumonia. His endocrine system was checked—were his hormones working properly? It seemed that this case, while looking like pneumonia, was actually quite different from pneumonia. But the search for a cause continued without any definite answers.

As Pauline entered Bill's room and looked at the monstrous bed that morning, she shuddered. It looked so inhumane! Yet she felt chastised. She should be grateful for it, shouldn't she? It was helping to save Bill's life. She went to him and touched his bare shoulder. It felt cold, and she shuddered again. She turned to a nurse. "Could you get a blanket for him, please?" she asked. "I can't stand to think he's so cold."

The nurse looked at Pauline sympathetically. "I understand, but we're actually trying to keep his body temperature cooler than normal while he's unconscious," she said. "It may help his recovery process." Pauline nodded in resignation, knowing the medical staff were doing their best.

Among the visitors that day were one of Bill's truck

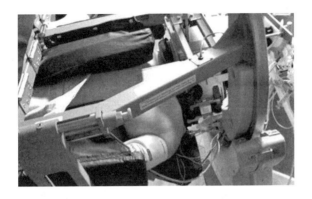

Only Bill's shoulder was exposed while in the prone
position. Pauline often prayed and touched him
here as the bed slowly made its rotation.

drivers and another of his siblings, Raymond Miller and
his wife, Ida, from Illinois. Eddie and Becky had to leave
that day, but it was difficult for them to tear themselves
away. They couldn't help wondering whether they would
soon be returning for a funeral.

That evening the church from Hicksville, Ohio, brought
supper to those keeping vigil for Bill. The Hicksville
church often associated with Bill and Pauline's church,
and their community just across the state line in Ohio was
not far from Fort Wayne. Their care touched Pauline and
brought warmth to her heart. She also received a call from
her Sunday school teacher, asking if the class could pray
for anything specific the next day in church. Gratefully,
Pauline mentioned her concerns about the business as
well as her desire to be submitted to God's will through
life, death, or a long recovery period.

. . . .

Another restless night came and went. When Pauline got back to the hospital at 8 a.m. on Sunday, December 29, she was greeted with sad news. Bill's fever had risen to 100.9. His oxygen saturation levels had dropped, and he needed to be in the prone position more of the time. It seemed he was getting worse, and they all knew he couldn't get much worse and survive.

Yet the puzzling fact remained that Bill's white blood cell counts were never elevated. A white blood cell count was one of the most typical indications of infection. So all the unknown "gunk" in his lungs wasn't actually an infection? This anomaly gave them a measure of hope, however small.

That morning they planned a short service at the hospital. One of the ministers was traveling to Ohio with his family and volunteered to stop at the hospital and lead a service for whoever was there. The crowd that gathered was enough for a small congregation. All the children and grandchildren were present, which brought a smile to Pauline's face. Floyd and Ruth's family was there, and several of Bill's siblings: Raymond and Ida, Geneva and Junior, and Dennis and Leanna from Arkansas, who had just arrived that morning.

The little group started the service with songs sung from memory. Following that, the minister read numerous portions of Scripture that spoke to their situation. Among the passages he read was Isaiah 43, and verses two and three became favorites for Pauline. She drank in the words:

> When thou passest through the waters, I will
> be with thee; and through the rivers, they shall
> not overflow thee: when thou walkest through
> the fire, thou shalt not be burned; neither shall
> the flame kindle upon thee. For I am the LORD
> thy God, the Holy One of Israel, thy Saviour ...

After reading from the Scriptures, the minister sat on the floor and read a story to the children. Following that, he asked if anyone had something to share. The time of honest sharing was bonding for the group. Although the words brought tears to Pauline's eyes, she felt grateful to hear them.

The third-floor waiting room saw many supporters that afternoon. People gathered and talked, laughed and cried. Bill's condition again stabilized a bit, with his fever breaking and his vital statistics slightly better. Pauline found out that after the morning service at church, the whole congregation gathered in a circle around the sanctuary, holding hands and praying for Bill. How comforting and supportive it felt to know that! Pauline felt assured God had heard their prayers and was working on Bill's behalf.

Monday morning dawned bitterly cold and snowy. *What a genuine winter!* Pauline thought as she made her way back to the hospital at 4 a.m. Bill's fever was gone, and he had tolerated the supine, or faceup, position in the bed for up to an hour at a time. That sounded like progress, but his numbers showed otherwise. The amount of oxygen needed and the pressure required for the oxygen to enter Bill's body stayed at alarmingly high levels. His X-rays also showed very little space in the lungs that was free of congestion.

Junior and Geneva had to go home that day. Before they left, the siblings all gathered around Bill's bed and sang *"Gott Ist Die Liebe,"* a well-loved German song from their earlier days. They began singing, but soon one after another felt the emotion of being gathered around their brother, possibly for the last time. When tears stopped several of them from singing, the song trailed off. They gave Junior and Geneva tearful goodbyes before dispersing.

A few minutes later Judith came to her mother with some interesting news. "Mom, the nurse told me she had to increase Dad's sleeping medication when you were singing! That means it stimulated him. He must have been able to hear you!"

"Oh, wow!" Mark said when he overheard. "That gives me an idea. Why don't we get some music for him to listen to?" And so saying, he fetched his computer and inserted a flash drive with music that could play beside his dad's bed.

They decided they needed to have a family council, so Pauline and her children gathered at 11:00 that morning to discuss schedules and business details. Norman took notes so they could refer to them later, and the discussion was helpful in making some plans. They decided to have the children rotate their visits to the hospital so they could all spend scheduled time with their own children and spouses as well.

As they went down to the first floor to get some lunch in the cafeteria, they met a group of ladies who had come to visit Pauline. One of them was Ruth Yoder, Pauline's friend who was also her twin. Pauline felt a pang of fear and disappointment as she looked at Ruth. What would happen this year on their birthday? They had a tradition of doing something together on that day, usually something that their husbands planned for them. This year they would turn sixty years old on April 29. They had hinted to their husbands that a big celebration would be nice. But now? Pauline's heart squeezed with anxiety. She couldn't dwell on that.

The ladies ate together in the cafeteria. Before they left, they stuffed Pauline's pockets with generous gifts of money. Pauline's smile was wobbly as she thanked them. "I feel so humbled by your kindness!" she exclaimed.

Evening brought little change to Bill's condition. "This just seems so endless," Pauline confided wearily to Judith. "How many days of this can we endure? I feel completely exhausted with the sameness of it all."

Judith nodded. "There's nothing to do but endure, Mom. I'll pray that God gives you all the strength you need."

CHAPTER SEVEN

Last Day of the Year

"Mrs. Miller, the ventilator tube has blown," the doctor pronounced solemnly. "It takes only ten seconds to replace it, but unfortunately, during that time your husband could go into cardiac arrest. Are you willing to let us do the procedure?"

"Doctor . . ." Pauline began hesitantly, "how bad is it, really? Is it worth changing the tube?"

"Well, I have to be honest and say that we are down to comfort care only by now," the doctor said. "There's really nothing more we can do for him. But the tube will need to be changed for there to be any hope of survival."

What turmoil of mind! Pauline's thoughts jumbled about, refusing to stay lined up and orderly. *Lord, really? A widow at fifty-nine years old . . . I don't want that, please! Oh, Lord, am I praying selfishly for your healing touch? And are you actually hearing the prayers of your saints?*

At last they decided to have the tube changed, but not until all the children could be gathered together. Around 4 p.m., everyone had come to the hospital. Judith's husband, who had been trained as a pharmacist, tried to encourage them all by reminding them that not all of Bill's bodily systems were declining. Only his lungs were failing; his heart, kidneys, liver, and brain were still functional. They should not lose hope until the rest of his body was declining. With this reminder, they felt better about going through with the changing of the tube. But they decided it would be best, in case the procedure would mark the end of Bill's life, to say goodbye to their husband and father.

It took so much strength to say goodbye. Pauline's entire being rebelled at the thought of releasing her husband. Finally, she forced herself to walk up to the RotoProne bed. She touched his bare shoulder. "Bill," she said with tears streaming down her face, "I release you to go be with Jesus if that's better. We don't want to see you suffer more in your sick body. You will get a new, glorious body!"

The children greatly struggled to say goodbye to their father as well. Some of them walked up to the bed and simply could not say anything. Turning around, they walked away. But they finally went back again and choked out their goodbyes.

Then everyone left the room except Tim and Judith. Being medically trained, they wanted to see the procedure being done. A few minutes later, they came out with relief on their faces. "His heart is still beating!" Judith exclaimed.

One huge hurdle had been overcome. Yet an even larger worry loomed directly in front of them. Bill could not be in the RotoProne bed much longer. Medical paralysis was necessary to be in the bed, and it was only safe to keep him paralyzed for a maximum of seven days. Tomorrow, New Year's Day, would be the seventh day he had been immobilized.

The church had to be notified, so Pauline forced herself to call the bishop and run a phone relay about Bill's condition. Bill's siblings were called, and several of them who had left to go home decided to come right back. The prognosis simply did not look hopeful.

A phone call was placed to Heiko and Sabine in Germany, and they wept at the thought of their dear friend being taken from them. They set about finding tickets to come to America, assuming the trip would probably be for Bill's funeral.

A few special friends stopped in that evening. One of them noted how Bill's skin was hanging from his bones; he had lost quite a bit of muscle mass already. Another friend said he would not go back and see Bill; it was better to remember him as he had been before the sickness.

Mark took his mother back to the hotel, where Pauline spent a long time praying and remembering. She remembered how many times Bill had helped other people plan their funerals; now she would have to plan his. She wondered why she hadn't been consistently kinder to her husband. Little annoyances that had previously bothered her certainly didn't matter in the face of death. When her sister Susan was on her deathbed, she had given some advice to those gathered with her. "When your husband asks you to go with him somewhere, just go," she had said. Pauline hadn't always followed that advice, and now she looked back with regret.

A faint smile crossed her face as she remembered how Bill could not seem to learn what clothing colors went together. He would put on shirts and pants that clearly were not meant for each other, and Pauline would sometimes ask him to change. She thought surely he would learn after a while, but Bill never seemed to get the hang of it. Finally she adopted a new policy. Each night she would lay out a shirt and pants for her husband to wear the following day. He loved the arrangement, and no more guesswork was involved!

But soon Pauline's pillow was wet with tears. She tried to focus on the verses God had given her in the last few days. *God will be with me,* she assured herself over and over until sleep overtook her.

CHAPTER EIGHT

The Miracle

Before dawn on the first day of 2014, Pauline awoke and got ready for the day. By 6:30 a.m. she and Mark were back at the hospital, where Pauline ate a nourishing omelet before going back to Room 3123. They found Bill in stable condition, with not much having changed in his vital statistics. People began to call and ask if they could come visit, so the family decided to allow staggered visits, minimizing overlap among callers.

During the morning, Mark stayed busy trying to find reasonable plane tickets for Heiko and Sabine and their two boys. They had found that the price for buying the tickets in Germany was prohibitive, but for some reason buying them Stateside made them less expensive. Finally the tickets were booked; the Kleins would be on their way soon!

The afternoon arrived with more decisions to be made. The nurse asked Pauline for permission to remove fluid from Bill's lungs. Pauline hesitated, thinking it sounded so invasive! She called Judith, who assured her that it was a normal procedure that wouldn't be particularly complicated. They wanted to do it before taking Bill out of the RotoProne bed, since it would take pressure off his lungs and potentially help them to recuperate better.

The moment arrived. Pauline signed permission for the fluid removal and left the room, knowing that after the procedure, Bill would be taken out of the bed that had enabled him to live for the last seven days.

They waited for about an hour, surrounded by a small support group in the waiting room. When they saw the nurse coming down the hall, she had a smile on her face. "We got only 100 CCs of fluid off his lungs!" she announced. "We thought there would probably be more, so this is a good sign. And we have him in a regular hospital bed now. Would you like to see him?"

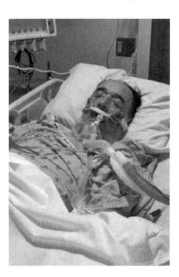

January 1, 2014: Bill's first day out of the RotoProne bed, but still heavily sedated.

Pauline didn't have to be asked twice! Gladly she hurried down the hall and into her husband's room. There he lay, no longer encased in a tube-like bed. He did not make a pretty picture, since his head, arms, and legs were swollen from his prolonged inactivity and prone position in the bed. But he was out, and he was still alive!

Everyone in the waiting area wanted to come back to see him, so they relaxed the rules a bit and brought them all to Bill's room at once. He was still unresponsive, but soon they would start taking him off the sedation medication. Only then would they know whether or not their Bill would come back to them. His chance of survival was still not clear, and they knew his brain might have been damaged from a lack of oxygen.

One of their visitors that evening said he had been studying Psalm 23 lately, and he had realized that "those who walk through the valley of the shadow of death" are not only those who are near death themselves, but also those who walk through the valley with them, caring for them. His words resonated with Pauline. She certainly felt she was walking through a long, dark valley. Yet God was with her, as the psalm said. She felt Him holding her up, helping her to function and to have faith and hope.

Throughout the evening they waited, fearing that Bill's oxygen saturation levels might decrease dangerously, but this time they didn't. Bill remained stable!

CHAPTER NINE

Awaking from the Long Sleep

Bill could see a face carved in the wooden pole. He was sure it was supposed to be the face of a holy man—a church leader. At the top of the wooden pole was a dim light, so dim it made the carport look eerie. Somehow he had found himself in a carport outside a funeral home in Elkhart, Indiana. He was alone, but gradually he became aware of a crowd of people in the darkness beyond the edge of the carport. They were whispering to each other.

Bill's eyes were riveted on the wooden face. Indeed, he seemed to be stuck fast in that position, right in front of the face. His arm gripped a rod that protruded from the pole right beside the carved head. Bill examined the head. It was perfectly chiseled; every hair was in place, and the beard was groomed to a perfect point. Every wood grain on the face seemed to speak of a highly educated man who felt very important.

Suddenly the wooden head began to move. Its lips smacked together, sounding like wooden sticks as it started to talk. With each smack of the wooden lips, the hair on the head rose and fell, as if to give importance to the words.

Bill watched the wooden head, horrified. Desperately he tried to get away from it, but he found his hand stuck fast to the rod protruding from the pole. The head continued to drone on. Bill began to pray earnestly in his mind, because his lips could not force out any words. Suddenly he heard a strong voice that he recognized. A minister from his church was proclaiming, "We have to go and pray for Brother Bill. He is in serious danger."

Within moments, Bill heard the minister's car come up behind him. The minister and his son jumped out of the car and came to stand beside Bill, one on either side of him. They began to pray earnestly for him. The minister's son noticed that Bill's hand was gripping the wooden rod and that he couldn't let go of it. When he prayed, he asked specifically that Bill be released from this thing that was binding him. Immediately the wooden head stopped its mechanical talking, and Bill's hand fell free of the wooden rod.

As Bill sank to the ground in relief, he could only think, *It was the prayers of the saints. That's the only thing that could give me freedom and release me from the powers of darkness.*

Another scene unfolded in Bill's subconscious mind. He was now in the country on a bright day, facing a large granary building. A railroad track ran close to the building, and on the train platform stood a crowd of people that Bill recognized. They were all talking anxiously about Bill—how sick he was and how they wondered if he would recover. Bill watched the crowd, sensing that someone would soon make an important announcement.

A man strode onto the platform. It was James Miller, a member of a neighboring congregation in northern Indiana. In a loud voice he said, "We just received word that Brother Bill Miller is very sick and that we need to pray for him." Everyone quieted down. They reverently bowed their heads as James prayed for Bill and his family. Bill watched, astonished, at something that happened in the granary every time James said Bill's name. A little door would open, and a handful of wheat flour would be thrown out of the granary, its puff dispersing far and wide. This was all happening for him and because of him! Bill didn't even try to stop the grateful tears welling up in his eyes.

Gradually the meaning of the vision dawned on Bill. All these people were "casting their bread upon the waters" (Ecclesiastes 11:1) as they interceded for Bill. But the granary was so full of wheat, and only a handful was thrown out at a time! More people needed prayer. Who would be willing to take up the task of caring for the innumerable souls who needed prayer? John 4:35 came to Bill's mind: "Lift up your eyes, and look on the fields; for they are white already to harvest." God's people were called to a great work! The prayers of the saints were even now healing Bill spiritually and physically so that he could answer the call of God to intercede for others.

. . . .

Bill could dimly hear Judith talking. What was she

saying? "Dad, this is your daughter, Judith. Open your eyes!" But his eyes felt so heavy that they simply wouldn't open.

"Squeeze my hand, Dad!" she commanded.

He moved his fingers and ever so slowly closed them around hers. Bill heard a collective gasp from several people around him.

"He did it! He squeezed my hand. He can hear us!" The excited voices rained down on his awakening consciousness. Then he heard his wife's voice and felt her hand stroking his head. He also recognized Norman's voice. Why was everybody surrounding him? Furthermore, why was he tied down on a bed? He couldn't move his arms or legs! And—horrors—something was in his mouth and going down his throat, and it felt awful.

Instead of waking up all at once, Bill woke up a little bit at a time as the medication was gradually reduced. He could understand what people were saying, but he couldn't speak with the respirator in his mouth. And they didn't give him much information, even though he had so many questions he couldn't voice.

"Do you know what's going on?" Judith asked him. All he could do was slowly shake his head to indicate he didn't. "Are you in pain?" she continued. He nodded.

The doctor prescribed a medication to help Bill relax, but it made him sleepier and less able to respond. As Bill continued to wake up, his puzzled frustration increased. People just weren't telling him what was going on! Later he learned that they wanted to shield him from too much overwhelming information at once. At the moment, however, Bill was tired of it all. As thoughts swirled around in his medicated head, one thought came to the forefront. *I will go home. I don't have to take this anymore.* And with that, he made a concerted effort to swing his legs over the side of the bed.

They moved only a few inches. They simply wouldn't go any farther. As he flailed his arms in desperation, he saw a nurse come to his bedside. "What do you want, Mr. Miller?" she asked sympathetically. "I see you're trying to get out of the bed. Do you want to leave and go home?"

Bill gave her a despairing look and nodded mutely. She looked at him with understanding in her eyes, and then she turned and slowly walked away. After a few moments, she seemed to have reached a decision. She turned back to the bed and looked Bill in the eye.

"For now, Mr. Miller," she said, "you'll need to stay here until you recover and get stronger. I understand that it's frustrating for you, but it's necessary for your own safety." She stopped but continued to gaze at Bill as if willing him to understand.

Bill reached out and patted the nurse's hand. It was all he could do, but it was enough. It communicated his acceptance and willingness to bear the ordeal he was facing. After that, hand patting became Bill's sign of approval and appreciation. He was gradually realizing he couldn't do one thing on his own—not even breathe. In this helpless state, he became more grateful for the people and the machines that were keeping him alive and helping him recover. He didn't like the feeling of the respirator hose in his mouth and throat, but he understood they were vital for his survival.

The more Bill woke up, the more he realized how many people were showing him love. Love pervaded his room, love sat in the waiting room, love blasted through the unseen spiritual places where prayers were prayed, and love worked in the homes of his family and community, where sacrifices were being made in his behalf.

Standing by his bed, Pauline looked down at Bill and saw tears running down his cheeks. It seemed he was feeling touched by the care being shown to him. She smiled. "It's okay, Bill. You know we really want to do all this for you because of how much we value and love you," she assured him.

CHAPTER TEN

The Long Recovery

*T*hey will be here soon! At least if they don't get stuck in this weather. Pauline kept watching the swirling snow outside the waiting room window. What a winter it was turning out to be! She shivered just looking at the snow. But Heiko and Sabine, along with their children, would be arriving soon. Friends were picking them up at the airport, and they would be coming directly to the hospital.

Their German friends arrived at 6 p.m. Pauline rushed to greet them in the waiting room. How wonderful it was that Bill was still alive, and they could see him!

"Oh, may we go see Bill right away?" Sabine asked.

"Most certainly," Pauline answered with a smile. "Come right this way." They headed down the third-floor hall and entered the room, but a nurse they didn't recognize stopped them.

"Are you family?" she inquired.

Pauline looked at her strangely. "Yes! This is my husband," she said with surprise in her voice.

"Okay, you can go in," said the nurse.

But the man looking up at Pauline from the bed was not Bill. With a sharp intake of breath, Pauline whispered, "Oh my, I . . . wonder if we have the wrong room?"

Such was the case. They beat a hasty retreat out of the wrong third-floor room and continued down the hall to Room 3123. With a sheepish smile, Pauline told Heiko and Sabine, "I'll probably laugh about this later. For now, I feel pretty embarrassed."

When Heiko and Sabine saw Bill, tears welled up in their eyes. "I'm so thankful we aren't at his funeral," Heiko whispered.

"Bill," Pauline spoke to her somewhat sedated husband, "Heiko and Sabine have come to see you. Do you understand?"

A tear trickled out of Bill's closed eye and down his cheek. He did understand!

Heiko offered a prayer for Bill in German. Then Sabine softly sang "What a Friend We Have in Jesus" in German. Pauline just smiled and cried. What a precious gift it was to have their German friends with them!

After the Kleins left to get settled in with their hosts for the week, Norman took his mother to the hotel and stayed with her that night. They talked at length, discussing their dawning hope along with the added questions. How long would this recovery take? Would Bill's brain function normally? What would the next season of their lives look like? Finally they realized they would be better off if they simply laid the questions aside and affirmed their trust in the blessed Controller of all things.

As Pauline went to sleep, she was struck with the thought of the sacrifices her son-in-law and daughters-in-law were making. They were keeping the home fires burning and allowing their spouses to spend a lot of time away from home to be with her and Bill. *I feel unworthy,* she thought, *but I'm so grateful for them and their unselfish sacrifices.*

. . . .

They woke up on the third of January to a thick layer of fresh snow. The temperature had dropped to five below zero. "I am chilled to the bone," Pauline told Norman with a shiver.

"Well, I don't think you have adequate clothing," Norman answered. "Shall we go shopping for some warmer things?" They went to Walmart, where Pauline was outfitted with a thicker coat and woolly accessories to cope with the bitter cold.

Upon returning to the hospital, Pauline discovered that Bill had digested a small amount of nutrition through the feeding tube in his stomach. His bowels were waking up, but slowly. Pauline noted the oxygen setting; it was down to 65 and the PEEP setting was at 15. Bill did not respond much that day, and a heaviness settled over Pauline. *What am I supposed to think?* she asked herself. *First I had to reconcile myself to the seemingly obvious truth that he was dying. Then he started getting better, which was great, but he's really not much better yet. He just lies there as if nothing has changed.*

The doctor had tried to prepare Pauline for the coming challenges. "Bill will probably not be able to work for months," he had said. "He might need to stay on oxygen for up to six months, and he will need to work a long time to get back the muscle mass that he has lost. It takes twice as long to regain muscle as it does to lose it. Also . . . we just don't know yet how his brain has handled all this oxygen reduction. It might turn out to be functioning normally, but there's a possibility it won't be."

All this weighed on Pauline's mind. She didn't know how she could be a help meet for a helpless husband. She steeled her mind and made herself think, *For now, he is still with us. That is a good thing, and it's the only thing I need to think about right now.* She tried to focus on the words of the song, "One Day at a Time, Sweet Jesus," and not allow herself to become overwhelmed.

· ·

More responses came the next day. The doctor told Pauline she could try to help Bill open his eyes. Gently she lifted the lid of one eye. "Bill, can you see me?" she asked hopefully. Slowly Bill's head moved up and down in a nod. Relief washed over Pauline. It was finally happening! His progress was measurable. Throughout the day they asked Bill questions and asked him to respond with different parts of his body. He could wiggle his toes. And his hand squeezes were getting noticeably stronger.

News was spreading that Bill's condition had changed and that he was waking up. Many people wanted to see the new and improving Bill, so a steady stream of visitors graced Room 3123. As the last of the visitors left that evening, they said, "Bill, can you tell us goodbye?"

In reply, Bill wiggled his toes, much to the amusement of all in the room.

. . . .

January 5 arrived, marking two weeks that Bill had been in the hospital. Since it was a Sunday morning, those gathered in Room 3123 had a short worship service. They all sang *"Wo Ist Jesus Mein Verlangen"* ("Where Is Jesus, My Desire"), which had been a German favorite of Bill's growing up. Bill's sister Geneva then read Psalm 103, which talks about the Lord healing our diseases and redeeming our lives from destruction. It was a psalm Bill would later request repeatedly to be read to him. They prayed around Bill's bedside, siblings' and spouses' hearts lifted in petition and thanksgiving to their heavenly Father.

Throughout the day, Bill woke up more and more. His arms and legs were tied to the bed to keep him from thrashing and pulling out his tubing, since he couldn't be expected to be thinking properly in his semi-conscious state. He seemed to be trying to say something to them. Of course, it took a lot of guessing, since he couldn't actually talk.

They got some paper and wrote down things they thought he might be trying to say. Bill would look at the paper and shake his head to everything they wrote down. Finally his brother-in-law Eddie said, "If I were him, I'd want to get out of this place." Bill began to nod his head with all his strength, even lifting it off the pillow.

Pauline looked at him compassionately. "Bill, you were very sick for a long time. That thing in your throat is a respirator that's breathing for you. You were so sick we thought . . . we thought you might not make it. You're getting better now, but you'll need to be patient because the doctor says it will take a long time to recover."

Bill's eyes grew larger. He understood, and her words surprised him. "Did you know it's the fifth of January, Bill?" Pauline went on. "You've been in the hospital for two weeks now." Bill shook his head a little, and tears began pooling in his eyes.

Between checking on Bill, the small group sat in the waiting room, putting a puzzle together and playing a game. Another storm had been predicted, and they watched it coming as they looked out the waiting room window. Huge flakes swirled down, faster and thicker. The temperature dropped.

Within a few hours they got word that the hospital would be going on Code White. That meant no medical personnel could leave and no new shifts could come in. The group quickly decided to bring their suitcases from the hotel to the hospital; rather be snowed in at the hospital than away from Bill. Potential visitors for the day were notified, and everyone decided to stay at home.

As the day wore on, the whole community went into lockdown mode. Only emergency vehicles were allowed on the road. The snow mounded into unbelievable piles as snowplows cleared the hospital parking lot unceasingly.

The little group at the hospital found it difficult to think of sleeping, and they weren't sure where they would all sleep anyway. They continued chatting and watching the proceedings from their third-story waiting room. Around midnight they noticed a string of snowmobiles coming toward the hospital. When someone inquired about it, they were told that people nearby had banded together to bring more nurses to the hospital! At least twelve new nurses arrived to relieve those who had been working overtime.

At last everyone settled down on any available couches or flat surfaces for a few hours of sleep.

. . . .

Bill was alert the next morning, but his frustration level increased along with his wakefulness. He was frustrated at the offensive tubing in his mouth, at the inability to do so much as swallow his own saliva, and at the nausea that assailed him when they tried to feed him formula through a feeding tube. Through the methods he used to communicate, Pauline understood that he desperately wanted her and other people to stay by his side. He seemed anxious and agitated.

Pauline didn't want to leave Bill's side that evening, but she was desperate for a good night of sleep. So, bidding him a reluctant fare-well, she made her way to the hotel through the frozen streets. The temperature had continued to drop, reaching fourteen degrees below zero by nightfall. Pauline thought wistfully of how Bill would be helping her step carefully on these icy sidewalks if he were with her. He would be helping to carry the

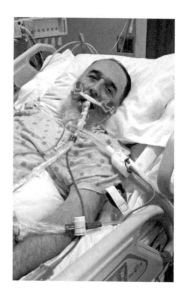

Awake at last, but still dependent on the respirator.

suitcases. And what if the van wouldn't start in the morning? If Bill were with her, he would know how to get it started again.

Pauline sighed wearily, hoping with all her heart she would have her husband back before long.

CHAPTER ELEVEN

Communication

Bill pointed to the letters and numbers on the sheet of paper, spelling out "Psalm 103."

"Sure, we'll read that for you!" Pauline said gladly. Just to have her husband cognizant and able to communicate was a treat, even if the method of communication was laborious.

Bill was understanding more and more about the gravity of his condition. When he saw his sister and brother-in-law from Georgia, he thought he was in a hospital in Georgia. It took some time for him to realize how many people had traveled to visit him in Indiana. Even Heiko and Sabine, along with their sons! Had they really come all the way from Germany just to see him in the hospital? Later he found out they had come expecting to attend his funeral. What a sobering thought!

Pointing again, Bill spelled "Dr. thought I dead." Then he followed up with "Pray," and "I have responsibility to tell the world about the power of prayer."

Suddenly a bout of nausea overtook him, and he began

throwing up bile. The nurses kindly cleaned him up, but getting the bile out of his beard was quite a process. "I'll get his beard trimmed," Pauline promised the nurses, who gave Bill medication to help calm his stomach.

A short time later Norman heard the nurses discussing whether or not to have Bill sit in a chair while they changed his bedding. One of the nurses thought they should wait a while longer because she wasn't sure Bill was ready to sit up. But Norman intervened, telling them, "I think if I were him, I'd want to sit in a chair like a man and look out the window." Bill heard him and was grateful.

So they complied. Bill was carefully placed in a chair, and cameras began clicking as family members rejoiced in his improvement. A photo was posted on the Internet, and the amazed comments poured in as word got around that Bill, no longer on the brink of death, was actually getting healthier!

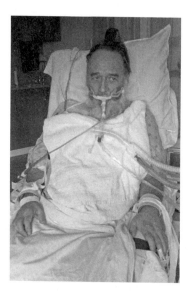

The first day on the chair!

Bill's chair time did help him to feel more like a man. He was able to give hugs and smile toothily for the cameras, even with the tube hanging out of his mouth.

His sense of humor seemed to be returning as well.

Bill communicated to Pauline that he wanted to see the RotoProne bed he had lain in for so long while he didn't know it. Pauline hesitated, wondering how it would affect him. When she finally showed him some pictures of the bed, Bill looked astonished, hardly able to believe he had been encased in that contraption for a whole week. How lifeless he looked in there!

In addition to pointing at letters to make words, Bill took a pencil and tried to write what he wanted to say. "You had visions from God?" Pauline asked as she read his scrawl. Bill nodded. "Why don't you tell us about them later when you can talk," Pauline suggested.

Another day in the hospital drew to a close. Pauline's heart was full of hope and joy as she retired for the night. Her theme for the day was Psalm 116:7–9: "Return unto thy rest, O my soul; for the LORD hath dealt bountifully with thee. For thou hast delivered my soul from death, mine eyes from tears, and my feet from falling. I will walk before the LORD in the land of the living."

The next day, January 9, would be Bill's sixty-second birthday.

. . . .

"I want everyone in the room," Bill scrawled.

"Are you sure you want everyone in here all at once?" Pauline asked.

"Yes. Pray and read Psalm 103." Bill was certain about

what he wanted this morning.

So they all piled in—Norman, Judith, Heiko and Sabine, Floyd and Ruth, a sister and an in-law, and several children. They read Scripture, prayed, and sang while Bill drank it all in. He could finally understand what was going on around him!

They celebrated Bill's birthday as best as they could, whether with him in his room or elsewhere. Heiko and Sabine brought a birthday cake for everyone to eat. Judith provided several homemade cakes for the nurses so they could celebrate their patient's birthday as well. Balloons, cards, and flowers decorated Room 3123. For a special memory that Bill could treasure later, Pauline recorded a group singing "Happy Birthday" for him.

Bill smiled, reveling in the love and care people showed him. But then reality set in, and his emotions crashed. The tubing in his mouth had caused thrush, and the pain was continuous and severe. He asked if they couldn't just take it out of his mouth, a query that was met with sympathetic looks but a firm "No." His whole body was still so weak, and his helpless feeling turned into hopelessness.

Pauline, sensing that he was getting depressed, tried to talk to him about it. Several of his children and in-laws in the room tried to give him answers to the frustrated questions he pointed out, but he didn't seem to take any comfort in that.

Finally he scribbled the words, "What's the use with life?"

His supporters became quiet as they contemplated how

to answer his question. Then they began speaking life-giving words.

"You don't realize how much you've progressed since coming to the hospital."

"You really are improving, and there will be an end to this hospital stay."

"Dad," his son-in-law Tim added, "you are surrounded by the love of many people who care about you deeply. That's the real reason for living—because you are loved, and you have love to give. You are a recipient of the very love of Jesus."

The words got through to Bill's heart. Tears spilled out of his eyes as he reached for his paper again. He crossed out the question he had asked; it had been answered.

Communication

CHAPTER TWELVE

Out of the Woods

Nights were long for Bill. At times he had trouble sleeping, and it seemed that as soon as he drifted off, someone in a brown lab coat would come in to take several vials of his blood. He knew it was necessary, but he never liked to see the brown-coated man come in, and he always liked to see him leave.

During the day, the diversion of visitors kept him sane. He felt an intense need for Pauline's comforting presence. When she was out of the room, he anxiously watched the clock and tried hard to be patient. When it seemed she had been gone for hours, he would look at the clock again and realize it had been only forty-five minutes.

Someone had the bright idea to play songs for Bill on the CD player. The first CD Pauline chose to play was made by Nelson Miller, a member of Pleasant Grove Church in northern Indiana. One song in particular spoke powerfully to them. It was called "I Weathered the Storm."

> *The thunder rolled, the lightning flashed, and it seemed
> all hope was gone;*

I stumbled on in the dark of night, afraid and all alone.
But a voice inside kept telling me to press onward toward the goal,
And now the clouds are giving way to the lights upon the shore.

Chorus:
'Cause I weathered the storm through the lonely night;
In the distance now, I see the morning light.
Yes, I weathered the storm through the lonely night;
Now I see the lights to my home on high.

I enter in through the golden gates, and I hear the angel choir;
I see the loved ones gone before, and I see my Savior smile.
The storm is gone, the night is past, and I've gone the last long mile;
And now I'll rest forevermore, as we gather 'round the throne.[1]

Tears gathered in Pauline's eyes as she thought, *Yes, we're weathering a storm too. And God is seeing fit to keep us on earth during this trial. But when we weather our last storm, we'll be in heaven!* She and Bill certainly had weathered numerous storms in their lives, and their current storm was the biggest one yet. But the songs continued, reminding them of what they knew was true: God was still bigger than all their storms. The music brought balm to Bill's soul, helping his mind to dwell on good things. He also

---

[1] Copyrighted by Nelson Miller. Used by permission.

slept better when the songs were playing.

The day after Bill's birthday, several of his visitors had to leave for home. Before they left, they came into his room to read more Scripture and pray. "What shall we read to you this time, Bill?" his sister Geneva asked.

Bill wrote out, "All of Psalm 119."

Geneva read the note to the group. They all paused for a moment, taken aback at the thought of Psalm 119's twenty-two sections. Then they saw the twinkle in Bill's eyes and burst out laughing. "He's coming back to us in full force!" Geneva said.

Overriding Bill's humorous request, his brother-in-law Eddie chose to read the considerably shorter Psalm 100. It reminded them that they were made by God, were the sheep of His pasture, and were under His watchful care. His mercy and His truth would last them their whole lives. Peace washed over Bill as he pondered the truth of God's care for him. He was still weak and in pain, but God was there with him, helping him to endure and infusing him with strength.

After the visitors left, the doctor came in with a much-longed-for announcement. "We would like to try taking your respirator out today, Bill," he said. "First we'll turn off the PEEP so it won't be forcing air into your lungs. Then we'll wait for an hour and a half to see if you can tolerate breathing on your own. After that, we'll see if we can take out the tubing." Bill's eyes shone with anticipation at the prospect.

An hour and a half later, a nurse came in and checked the numbers on Bill's monitors. She left the room for a moment, and when she came back in, she said, "We're going to take it out now, Bill. Here we go!"

Almost before Bill comprehended what was happening, the hated tube had slipped out of his throat. His first hoarse words were, "Praise God." What an amazing gift it was to talk again!

"Please try not to talk," the nurse implored him earnestly. "Your vocal cords need to rest for twenty-four hours after the tubing is removed. You could do more damage to them if you talk."

Her warning made little impression on Bill. He could talk, and he *would* talk. "I am extremely hungry," he announced. "Any chance there's food around here?"

Granddaughter Janessa uses a silly putty stethoscope . . . after the respirator was removed.

The nurse looked at him sympathetically. "We have to wait thirty-six hours after the respirator is taken out before you may have food," she answered. "Any food or liquid can hurt those vocal cords and get into your lungs, which we definitely don't want. You won't starve as long as you're on IV."

With a sigh, Bill rested against his pillows. Soon he made them aware of another need he had. "My mustache," he rasped. "It feels like wires poking into my nose."

"I'll have Norman bring a razor this afternoon," Pauline promised.

Norman willingly complied. It took a while for the stiff hairs to be tamed by the shaving cream so they could be shaved off. After Norman had painstakingly prepared the hairs and maneuvered his razor laboriously under his father's nose, the offensive hairs were removed. When he was done, Bill whispered with a smile, "Now that's a mustache according to Bill's standard."

That night, Bill lay awake. Whether it was from excitement or some sort of medication in his system, he didn't know. The doctor eventually decided to give him Xanax to help him calm down, but unfortunately, the only effect it had was to make Bill a little loopy.

Around 1 a.m., Bill needed to go to the restroom. A bedpan was available, but he did not appreciate its company. He felt he could get up and go to the restroom by himself, so he swung his weak legs over the side of the bed. As he began to scoot off the bed, Bill realized his IV tubes were getting tight. The jumbled mess resisted all his efforts to disconnect the tubes. He tried to stand, only to find out his legs simply wouldn't support him. Nor could he get back into his bed. There he was, sliding slowly to the floor, unable to stop his fall. His mind finally made one good decision—he called for the nurse.

Nurse Jodi came quickly, sized up the situation, and kindly asked him if he needed help. "I sure do," Bill humbly replied. "I'm sorry . . ."

"Don't worry about it, Bill," Jodi assured him. "You didn't really know what you were doing. Xanax can do things like this to a person."

After she got him back into bed, he dozed for a few hours. But the next thing he knew, he awoke to the sound of himself shouting and howling, trying to get his legs out the other side of the bed.

Nurse Jodi calmed him down quickly again, but she could see Bill was embarrassed. Later he confided to Pauline, "Don't overdose on drugs. They can ruin your Christian testimony quickly." The corners of Pauline's mouth twitched as she thought of the scenes her husband had created in his mind-altered state.

The thirty-six hours finally passed. Bill said he was ready to post a sign saying, "Will work for food." But at last the food came. Bill asked a blessing over it and was struck with the usually routine words, "Please strengthen our bodies with this food." Now he really meant it. He felt like a new child of God as he communicated out loud with his heavenly Father.

Then he tasted the chicken noodle soup. With each tiny swallow of broth, strength seeped back into Bill's muscles. He was still so weak that Pauline had to feed him for several days, yet he could feel himself getting steadily stronger. Soon he could impress his visitors by touching his nose and lifting his legs. Although they seemed like such small acts, they took so much effort for a man who had hardly moved a muscle for two weeks.

But only two days after he started ingesting food again, Bill came down with a fever. The doctor said a tiny trickle of water must have seeped through the damaged vocal cords and entered his lungs. To prevent that from happening again, Bill would need to swallow water in a careful way, taking a sip and then tucking his chin down while he swallowed. That helped all the water to end up at the right place. It took a long time to swallow this way, up to fifteen minutes per glass of water. And Bill had to drink as much water as possible to give his muscles fuel to build themselves up again.

As inconvenient as recovery was, Bill was still exuberantly grateful. He had not needed to go back on the respirator! He was still getting oxygen through a nasal cannula, but that wasn't so bad. And whenever he began to get depressed because of his situation, he remembered the day Tim had reminded him how much he was loved. He clung to that thought, and it gave him mental strength in much the same way as nutrition was giving him physical strength.

CHAPTER THIRTEEN

Sixth Floor

"Hello, Bill! Physical therapy here," a young man announced as he entered the room. "We're going to help you do exercises that will strengthen your muscles and let you get back to your normal life sooner." So saying, he took Bill through a series of exercises, showing him how to move his joints and limbs for maximum effectiveness.

When the doctor came in, he told Bill, "If you keep improving at this rate, we just might be able to move you out of ICU tomorrow."

Amazing, Pauline thought. *The improvements just keep coming.*

It seemed everyone wanted to come and see this "miracle man." Many visitors trickled in and out of Room 3123, and Bill enjoyed them all. Even though he exercised his vocal cords a little too much, his voice did grow stronger as the day wore on.

When night came, the family traded roles again, as was their custom. They had been taking turns staying with Bill, sleeping at home, and sleeping at the hotel. This time it was

Tim and Judith who stayed at the hospital, while Norman and Sharon went home to sleep at Bill and Pauline's house. Pauline settled in at the hotel.

As Pauline lay in bed, processing the day as she usually did at night, her primary feeling was grateful praise for God's goodness and mercy to Bill and her. She also had to ponder why God had healed Bill when He hadn't chosen to heal others. In their church alone, she could think of four people who no longer had their spouses. She knew she didn't have any more reason to need her partner than they had, and she knew she was no better or more deserving than they were. God's ways were simply past finding out. She could only accept the fact that she had been the recipient of God's mercy for an unknown reason.

. . . .

On Sunday, January 12, Bill ate his breakfast as ravenously as a man in his condition could. He thought the yogurt, bran muffin, and oatmeal were fit for a king.

A chest X-ray taken that morning revealed noticeably fewer cloudy areas. Where was the "gunk" going? There really was no clear explanation, but they were grateful nonetheless.

Around 10:00 in the morning they began the process of moving from one room to another. Pauline and the other family members took all the cards off the wall and gathered their personal belongings. They looped tubing into neat circles and said goodbye to the nurses who had cared for Bill so well during his most critical time. At long last the bed was rolling through the halls on its way to the sixth floor.

A few doors down, Bill glanced into a room and noticed the RotoProne bed in use. "Is that where I was?" he asked incredulously.

An unbidden sob caught in Pauline's throat. "Yes," she said simply.

Bill gazed at the machine for a moment, thinking of his long week of sleep inside the coffin-like machine. He could picture his family and friends standing around it, praying for him and anointing him, coming to grips with the possibility of losing him. He shuddered involuntarily. "It seems like holy ground . . . but I can't look at it anymore," he whispered.

On they rolled to his new room, with a new nursing staff. Norman was preaching at Pleasant Grove that morning, so after they got settled in, they called the church's phone to listen in on the sermon.

For lunch, Bill feasted on a Turkey Manhattan. He was still too weak to feed himself, but Pauline heartily enjoyed feeding him. It was such a relief to be able to do things for him after seeing him comatose for so long!

Tim and Judith had stayed in the area overnight with their two sons. But the boys had begun to succumb to viruses, with Bryce coughing and Trenton having nausea, so they decided to go home shortly after lunch. Before they left, they came into the room to tell Bill goodbye.

When Bill saw them, he was amused to see Trenton's little head swathed in a face mask. "I didn't want to spread any germs, *Dawdy* (Grandpa)," Trenton said.

"Well, thank you for coming to see me," Bill said. "Now just go home and rest up and get well soon!"

That afternoon many visitors showed up again. Two little girls, Briana and Shianne Nissley, brought their Sunday school offering money for Bill. "We took an offering for you because we wanted you to have more money," Briana explained seriously.

The total was $100.49. Bill just shook his head, rendered speechless by the care of the children in his church. Briana went on. "We prayed for you too. All of us in our class, and we—" she pointed to Shianne and herself—"we prayed for you at home too. Every night before we went to bed."

"Thank you," Bill said earnestly, his eyes filling with tears. "That means so much to me."

After they left, Pauline commented, "Just think of how many children were praying for you through this whole ordeal. I'm sure the Father heard each one of their prayers, and I'm sure it moved Him to work on your behalf."

That day Bill began to take his first slow, hobbling steps, with a little help from the nurses. As Pauline watched him mince along the floor, she was struck with how the skin hung from his body. An astonishing amount of muscle mass was simply not there anymore. Bill had also lost thirty-four pounds—a lot to lose in a short time. He looked too much like photos she had seen of prisoners from

World War II prison camps, emaciated skeletons of their former selves. Yes, the road to recovery would be long, but at least it was happening!

. . . .

After Bill's first night of sleep on the sixth floor, Dr. Israbian visited and assessed him. Earlier he had told Bill he would be coughing up a lot of yellow mucus as the pneumonia healed. To his surprise, Bill had not needed to cough much at all. However, now as the doctor visited, Bill did cough up some mucus. Dr. Israbian inspected it carefully, noting that it was completely clear. He was quiet for a moment. Then, looking Bill in the eye, he stated, "Mr. Miller, you never had pneumonia. This is not something a pneumonia patient would cough up."

Before they could ask the obvious question, *Then what did he have?* the doctor went on. "Here's what I think happened. It's my best guess, but I don't know for sure. I think you had bronchitis to begin with, and your body responded to the Bactrim you took to help you fight the bronchitis. Then, for some unexplainable reason, I think your immune system went haywire and started attacking your body instead of helping it. Your body released all the chemicals, and they infiltrated your lungs. It was a bit like an auto-immune disorder in which cells destroy each other—only in your case it was a one-time attack instead of a constant struggle in your body. The reason I think this is what happened is that nothing grew on the cultures.

There is simply no evidence of you having a disease."

Dr. Israbian continued, giving them the likely prognosis. "You may need to be on oxygen for six months, and your total recovery will likely take a whole year. I think, though, that your health will return to what it once was. Oh, I don't think you'll be running any marathons!" he said with a laugh. "Also, we're not sure yet if your lungs will ever function at full capacity again. Only time will tell with that. But I think you'll continue to improve, especially if you do enough therapy."

"Do you think it would be okay for someone to come to our house to do therapy?" Pauline asked hopefully. She was so ready to have Bill home again.

"Well, to be honest, I think he'll improve much faster if you have him at a facility where his therapy can be more regular than if he's at home," the doctor replied. "He'll become fully functional more quickly."

Just before he left, the doctor strongly recommended that Bill should get an annual flu shot and a pneumonia vaccine, since he was prone to respiratory issues.

Bill watched the figure retreating through the door and sighed. "He did a lot for me," he told Pauline. "I sure am grateful for his care. But I tell you," he added firmly, "if the doctors didn't really know what I had and were possibly treating me for the wrong thing, and I still got better . . . I think that is a testimony of the power of God. I think God wanted to show Himself strong to us, and to do that, I had to be sick with a mysterious illness only He could heal!"

That afternoon Tim and Judith came to help them decide where to go for physical therapy. They decided on The Maples, a facility with a reputation for quality care. The best part was that The Maples was only ten miles from their home. What a treat that would be! And he would be going there sooner than they had anticipated. The doctor said it could be the very next day.

CHAPTER FOURTEEN

On to The Maples

"I can't remember the last time I was this close to the ground," Bill commented as he gazed with fresh eyes at the melting snow piles whizzing past the car window. It was January 14, and they had just left the hospital and were speeding toward The Maples, where a cozy room awaited Bill.

Pauline thought of how good it had felt to push Bill in a wheelchair out of Parkview North and across the parking lot to the waiting car. Was it possible that just a few weeks ago she had heard the doctor's voice saying, "There's nothing

Leaving the hospital at last!

more we can do for him"? Now her husband was leaving the hospital, alive and improving!

Room 214 at The Maples became Bill's new temporary home. With its glowing lamps and soft carpet, the atmosphere was much more comfortable than the stark hospital room had been. Pauline took pleasure in feeding Bill his supper before she went home to sleep in her own bed for the night.

Therapy began, and Bill discovered he had never realized how many different types of muscles he had. Not only did he have to learn the best ways to strengthen his arms and legs, he also had to strengthen his throat muscles. He had to take speech therapy to strengthen his swallowing muscles so he wouldn't get water in his lungs again. It took a lot of effort, but Bill gave it all he had. He decided that since he had to do therapy anyway, he would try to have fun with it. He joked with the therapists until they were all laughing.

And he improved! On his third day at The Maples, he walked fifty feet with the walker. The next day he walked one hundred feet. And the following day, he doubled his record again and walked two hundred feet!

"Your recovery seems almost miraculous to me," one therapist commented.

Her colleague nodded. "We don't see progress this fast very often at all," she added.

Bill and Pauline decided to set a goal of being at The Maples for only two weeks. It actually seemed possible.

He started to feed himself shortly after he arrived, and then he could take a shower by himself. His sore mouth started feeling better as well, which made eating more pleasurable. His muscles often ached with fatigue, but the ache reminded Bill of muscles that were working

Therapy at The Maples was fun.

and being restored.

Visitors arrived every day. With The Maples being much closer to Bill and Pauline's home community, people were thrilled with the convenience of being able to see their friend. One evening the youth group came to visit. Each person had prepared something for Bill: cards, notes, poems, cookies, and other little packages. They told him he could open two cards a day until he had opened them all. They also sang for him, which sounded like heavenly music to his ears.

That evening, Shawn, one of the young men in the youth group, told Bill something he would always treasure. "I suppose they told you about the time our whole church stood in a circle and held hands and prayed for you?" he asked. Bill nodded, smiling. It had been during the time he was unconscious in the RotoProne bed. "Well, it really did something for me too when we joined together and prayed for a miracle for you," Shawn went on. "I felt bonded to the church like never before. It increased my faith and my love for the people in our church."

Bill smiled broadly. "I'm so glad," he said. "That's one of the ways God used my sickness for good. It increased people's faith."

· ·

One day Bill and Pauline were talking about more of what had happened while Bill was in the RotoProne bed. "I don't think I've told you about all the visitors you had during that time," Pauline told her husband. "Did you know that Jason came to visit once?"

"He did?" Bill asked incredulously. "Amazing!" Jason was a former employee of Bill's who had left the company on rather bad terms. Their strained relationship had been a source of grief for Bill.

"Yes, and he even walked right up to the bed and prayed for you!" Pauline exulted.

Bill just shook his head. "Praise God," he said. "He is using my sickness to bring about more good than I ever dreamed of!"

"So, the visions you had," Pauline continued, "do you think they had specific messages for you?"

"Definitely," Bill answered with conviction. "The more I think about them, the more it becomes clear to me.

The vision of the wooden head—" he shuddered a bit as he remembered it—"had several implications. My hanging onto that rod, unable to let go, made me realize I was somehow connected to the sinful world and its works of darkness. I think I may have been imbibing and accepting some ideas I wasn't even aware of. And it showed me that whether our sicknesses are spiritual or physical, the prayers of the saints are powerful to break that bondage."

Pauline nodded in understanding. "And the granary with its puffs of grain going out every time they said your name?" she asked.

"That just has a clear missionary message for me," Bill said. "It says again that prayer is powerful, but beyond that, it tells me of the many people whose souls need prayer. They need to hear about God's power. I used to be pretty shy when it came to talking about God to strangers, but I don't feel so much reticence now. I feel a lot bolder."

Pauline smiled. She wasn't just getting her old Bill back—she was getting a new, more spiritually in-tune husband as well.

. . . .

A few days after he moved to The Maples, Bill noticed an unwelcome development. One evening the children and grandchildren came to eat pizza together. Bill enjoyed their company, but he began hearing an annoying ringing in his ears. On and on it went, like a mosquito that would never leave. It seemed to intensify when a loud hubbub of voices

Grandsons Bryce and Trenton
enjoy rides at The Maples.

went on around him, and it grated on his nerves. The worst noise for him to tolerate was whining or wailing children, even if they were his own grandchildren. Saddened, he had to ask the group to keep things quiet. When he couldn't take it anymore, Pauline took him back to his room for some solitude. It was just more evidence of what his body had been through and how much it still needed to heal.

To pass the time, Bill listened to music and began to read. He felt encouraged to be able to use his mind again and form cohesive thoughts. He could read the Bible for about thirty minutes at a time. More time than that gave him a headache, so he tried to rest his brain quite a bit as well.

Sometimes his visitors brought him interesting things

to read. One poem by an unknown author spoke volumes to Bill when a friend from church brought the poem in for him.

> When an accident or illness
> Makes us step aside to heal,
> There's an added complication—
> The frustration that we feel.
>
> "This doesn't fit my schedule, Lord!"
> (We piously complain);
> "There's so much work to do for you!
> This time is spent in vain!
>
> "I can't see why you'd want me
> To be set aside this way."
> But the Master interrupts us,
> And we hear Him gently say,
>
> "Every trial has a limit
> That I've set by mine own hand,
> And the time required for healing,
> Just as surely I have planned.
>
> "If I truly am the Master,
> Then I have the right to say
> That the work belongs to others
> And that you should rest today!
>
> "You've been a faithful servant,
> But I'm drawing you apart
> So that I can sit beside you
> And speak softly to your heart.

"There are things I want to say that
You won't hear unless you're still;
There's a strength that comes from resting,
That you will need to do my will.

"So instead of feeling badly
That you must inactive be,
Just enjoy this gift of quietness
And spend some time with me!"

Bill read the poem over and over. He took its message to heart. "Lord," he would pray, "please speak to me about what job you have for me to do right now, and what job you're preparing me for in the future. I want to do your will."

And he did hear from God. Often it was a passage of Scripture or a spiritual concept God wanted to impress on him. Most often the words found in Matthew 22:37–39 came to his mind: "Love the Lord thy God with all thy heart, and with all thy soul, and with all thy mind. This is the first and great commandment. And the second is like unto it, Thou shalt love thy neighbor as thyself." Bill had been a recipient of much love from many people, and he felt compelled to love others now with his whole heart. The more he read and pondered about the deep love of God, the more he felt called to speak to people about God and His love. "Lord, use me as you choose, and help me to love you and my neighbors more," became his constant prayer.

Only eight days after he had been admitted to The Maples, the staff decided to do a home evaluation on

Bill. That meant he would go home for a few hours and see how he would do there. Bill and Pauline excitedly climbed into the car to go home *together*. There they met the therapist, who saw to it that the house was suitable for Bill's needs. They even had Bill sit in his office chair and pretend he was dispatching trucks. After eating chili together, they left for The Maples again with thrilling news from the therapist: Bill would be able to come home for good only two days later, on Friday, January 24. That would be a full four days earlier than their optimistic goal of a two-week stay!

A compact oxygen concentrator unit came along with them as they packed up their belongings. It was small

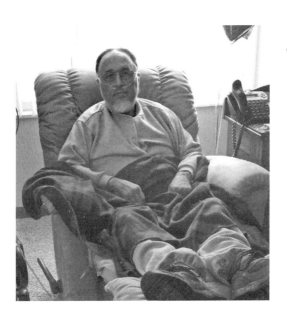

Home at last!

enough to be set on Bill's walker so he could take it with him wherever he went. They said goodbye to The Maples in yet another snowstorm, and Norman capably drove them home.

The house was wonderfully clean, having had Sharon's expert touch applied to its surfaces. She had also prepared supper for them, which they ate gratefully. After supper, Bill sat in his favorite recliner, relaxing. He reached for the Bible on the stand beside his chair, opened it, and began to read. Pauline just watched her husband in silent gratitude. So often in the past weeks she had wondered if Bill would ever sit there again. What a welcome sight he was!

That night Bill occupied his side of the bed again. Pauline went to sleep with a smile on her face.

CHAPTER FIFTEEN

Follow-up

"Dad?" Mark's voice came through the doorway. "It's true . . . you're actually sitting there, awake! I can hardly believe it." He held his dad in his arms and let the tears come. Mark and Norma and their family had just come from Ohio. It was the first time they had seen Bill fully awake since his illness, and the relief brought a wave of emotions.

All the children and grandchildren planned to spend several days together, enjoying each other's company in the same house. They convened on Saturday, a day after Bill had come home from The Maples. Beginning an immediate celebration, they chattered happily, played games, and ate.

They had planned to go to church together on Sunday, but another snowstorm blew in and prevented even short-distance travel. So they made the best of being snowed in together—until a bump in the road brought new anxiety.

Several children in the household started with fevers

and stomach viruses, and a few adults felt touched by the bug as well. It was inconvenient having sick children, but mostly they were concerned about Bill. They tried to keep the sick ones as far away from him as they could, but they knew Bill's weakened immune system might pick up any viruses within shouting distance.

However, Bill only kept getting stronger and healthier. After a few days, they were all well again, and Bill had not caught the bug! They praised the Healer once more.

. . . .

Three and a half weeks passed. During that time, Bill noticed that he was losing hair at a higher rate than he had in the past. The ringing in his ears and his sensitivity to noise did not decrease. But in spite of these annoying symptoms, he felt stronger and more mobile every day. He did his exercises faithfully, pacing through the house with his walker, doing arm stretches, and doing leg lifts with weights.

Norman and Sharon had stayed on, offering physical help and emotional support to their recuperating father. Norman kept in touch with the work at Northern Youth Programs, doing some administrative work via email and telephone. On one such phone call, something clicked with the NYP airplane mechanic on the other end as Norman described his father's illness. "It sounds just like blastomycosis!" the mechanic said.

Blastomycosis, Norman learned, was a fungal disease.

The fungus was especially prevalent in the area around Dryden, Ontario. It lived in moist soil and rotting wood. Some people who inhaled it exhibited no adverse symptoms, but others were affected strongly. Symptoms often took several months to appear, with the first symptom usually being respiratory distress. It was often mistaken for pneumonia.

Interested, Norman researched the disease and talked about it with his parents. Bill had been working with the soil when he visited NYP the summer before, and his symptoms had slowly come on during the following months. He had exhibited nearly all the symptoms of blastomycosis except the skin lesions that usually occurred in patients. They decided to call the doctor and tell him about their findings before their follow-up visit, allowing the doctor to research the possibility himself.

When they visited Dr. Israbian on February 18, he watched Bill walk into the room and exclaimed, "You look mighty good for a man we thought was dying!" Then he showed Bill and Pauline the results from all the cultures and tests, including one for the blastomycosis fungus.

All the results were negative. Tests for four different fungi, plus a host of viruses and bacteria—all negative. According to the tests, Bill hadn't been sick with any of them! The doctor reiterated that he thought it was the immune system attacking the body like a one-time atomic bomb.

Bill's lung capacity and functionality were checked while they were there, and the results came back even better than they had hoped for. Again they lifted their hearts in wonder and praise to the God who was still performing miracles on their behalf. Dr. Israbian also had Bill walk the halls at a fast pace for six minutes in order to check Bill's oxygen level at the end of physical activity. It came in at 94 percent. The doctor was amazed. "You don't need the supplemental oxygen machine anymore, Mr. Miller," he stated. "And we thought you might need it for six months!"

Lung X-rays were taken, and they showed a small infiltration at the bottom of the lungs. "That could just be scar tissue," Dr. Israbian surmised. "The lungs are quite clear. I really don't know what happened to all the secretions that were in there. You never coughed much up, which is surprising.

"To conclude our consultation here," the doctor went on, "I want you to use a CPAP machine for your sleep apnea. Otherwise, I don't need to see you for a whole year!"

Bill and Pauline went on their way rejoicing.

CHAPTER SIXTEEN

Vitamin D Therapy

"We think you should go to Arizona," Norman told his parents.

Judith nodded. "It's been so cold around here for so long, and with your lung issues, we think a warmer climate would help you heal," she added.

The idea seemed a little frivolous to Bill and Pauline, but the thought of relaxing in warm sunshine did sound attractive. They finally decided to visit the southwestern state for two weeks.

They flew down on February 27 and settled into a house in a nice neighborhood where they already had some acquaintances. Bill got out and walked as often as he could, although he had to keep his walks brief. His strength improved daily, and he even tried to play cornhole with his neighbors a time or two. Pitching the little bags of corn into a hole in a board some distance away gave him good exercise, but the sport took quite a bit of energy for his recovering muscles. After a few throws, he was content to sit back and watch while the others continued.

The sunshine worked wonders on Bill's health. Every day he could take longer walks. One day as he was walking along Eva Street, he noticed a house for sale. His heart started beating faster. *What if we could buy a house down here and live in it when we get older? We could rent it out to snowbirds until we're ready to move.*

He discussed the idea with Pauline, and the more they talked about it, the more they were excited by the possibility. After making some inquiries, they concluded that God was indeed opening doors for them to buy the Eva Street house. They went back home after two weeks in Arizona, but they made plans to come back in April to close on the house.

During their time in Arizona, Bill started a new habit of eating about a dozen M&Ms every day. Their little pop of flavor seemed to be just the pick-me-up he needed. A few weeks after starting the practice, he noticed something surprising. "Pauline!" he announced one day. "I'm not losing hair anymore. You don't think my comfort food snack has anything to do with that, do you?"

"Hmm . . ." said Pauline with a smile. "I suppose it could have. Your diet hasn't really changed otherwise. I'd be a little surprised if chocolate could stop hair loss, but I guess anything is possible."

"I know a few men in church who should try it as an experiment," Bill said with a mischievous gleam in his eye. "Depending on their results, I might want to buy shares in the M&M company."

Pauline chuckled. Her husband's sense of humor still delighted her.

. . . .

When they got back to Indiana, the weather was finally milder. Bill was still improving, but scars remained. The ringing in his ears never quite went away, and when he was in crowds or hearing other grating noises, he had to wear ear plugs or get away to a quieter place. The soles of his feet had developed a marked tenderness as well. He couldn't stand for long periods at a time.

Bill's job was calling him, and he was eager to get back to dispatching his trucks full-time. By the end of April, he was trying to do all the dispatching himself. He found that he had to take at least one break every afternoon to nap or rest for a while. If he didn't, he would develop debilitating headaches.

Sometimes Bill felt he couldn't take the mental strain of thinking so much while dispatching. He made a few mistakes and forgot some important details every so often. Yet he kept on, feeling the responsibility to manage his business as best he could.

CHAPTER SEVENTEEN

Emotional Amnesia

Bill drove down Route 30, a road he had traveled many times throughout his life. But nothing looked familiar to him this time. He consulted his GPS. Yes, it said he was on Route 30, so surely he was. *I guess I have to rely on this thing to get me where I want to go,* Bill thought. *I sure can't make sense of my route.*

It was odd, this unfamiliar disconnect between what he used to know and what he knew now. Sometimes things made sense to him, but at other times he would look at a once-familiar landmark such as his own house and feel no sense of connection to it at all.

The most disturbing aspect of Bill's amnesia was his occasional disconnect from his wife. In his head he knew he was married to Pauline, that they had shared many experiences together, and that he loved her—but sometimes his feelings and his memory didn't match with the facts. He would look at Pauline and feel a blank, as though there had never been any history with her at all.

One day as he sat in his office chair, he blurted out,

"Sometimes I just don't know who I am."

Pauline cocked her head and gave him a sympathetic glance. "What do you mean? We all know you are Bill."

"But I don't feel a connection with my memory of who I was in the past and who I am today," Bill tried to explain.

Pauline was saddened when Bill couldn't connect with people or places in his mind and heart. She knew it was probably because his brain had been oxygen-starved, and she reminded herself that the aftereffects could have been a lot worse. During this time, she found a book that greatly helped her perspective on Bill's issue. In her book, *The Long Awakening,* Lindsey O'Connor related her story of coming out of a forty-seven-day coma following a traumatic childbirth. She talked about how, despite the happiness her husband and family expressed about her recovery, she could not connect with her past self or her past relationships. As Bill and Pauline voraciously read O'Connor's memoir, they felt a strong connection with someone who had gone through a similar experience and found herself again. It gave them hope for the future.

. . . .

"Sometimes during recovery I got a picture in my mind of God and Jesus having a conversation," Bill told his audience at the small Mennonite church. "I heard Jesus saying, 'Father, I hear something rising from the earth. Many people from Germany to California are continuing in prayer for a certain man named Bill Miller. They have already anointed him in faith, unto healing and the forgiveness of sins. Also, there is this sweet-smelling savor rising up from the small congregation where Bill is a member. They are all in a circle, holding hands and asking for the God of heaven to look down and answer their pleas and heal Bill's body. Father, this is all happening in their weekly prayer meeting. These people, his friends in Germany, and many other friends and relatives, have requested a special time of prayer for this man. Some of the hospital staff are also praying. Would you consider healing him so that all these people will praise your holy name? Would you consider this because of your love for this brotherhood?'

"The Father said, 'Yes, I will heal him, but first I will test the faith of the family and the brotherhood a few more days.'

"These are just some of my earthly thoughts," Bill continued, "and my desire is to draw our attention to our great God."

Bill had been asked to share his story with a local group of believers, which he did willingly. So many people needed to be encouraged in their faith and in their prayer lives. He wanted to fulfill his calling of using his testimony to increase people's faith in their all-powerful God, so he spoke whenever he got a chance.

"My experience was not a pleasant one," he concluded near the end of his talk, "but as Job 2:10 says, 'What? shall we receive good at the hand of God, and shall we not receive evil?' Sometimes we receive that which seems to be evil, but we need to keep those experiences in perspective by holding onto the truth of Romans 8:28: 'And we know that all things work together for good to them that love God, to them who are the called according to his purpose.' God has worked out good because of what He took me through, and He continues to do so with each new day He gives me."

Afterword

Many stories in the Bible speak of the healing power of Jesus. One vivid example comes from Acts 9:36–42:

Now there was at Joppa a certain disciple named Tabitha, which by interpretation is called Dorcas: this woman was full of good works and almsdeeds which she did. And it came to pass in those days, that she was sick, and died: whom when they had washed, they laid her in an upper chamber. And forasmuch as Lydda was nigh to Joppa, and the disciples had heard that Peter was there, they sent unto him two men, desiring him that he would not delay to come to them. Then Peter arose and went with them. When he was come, they brought him into the upper chamber: and all the widows stood by him weeping, and shewing the coats and garments which Dorcas made, while she was with them. But Peter put them all forth, and prayed; and turning him to the body said,

Tabitha, arise. And she opened her eyes: and when she saw Peter, she sat up. And he gave her his hand, and lifted her up, and when he had called the saints and widows, presented her alive. And it was known throughout all Joppa; and many believed in the Lord.

As it happened in Joppa, I want it to happen here. My desire is that those who read my story will believe in God. May those who already believe in God come to believe in Him more fully, and may those who are struggling to have faith at all be encouraged to believe in God's reality.

I know my work is not done yet. But, brothers and sisters, your work isn't done yet either. I want us all, both young and old, to work together in the work of God's kingdom, in love and in honor preferring one another. We need to continue in prayer and supplication, building each other up and earnestly contending for the faith that was delivered to us. I want us to run with patience the race that is set before us, both here in America and abroad, wherever God leads each of us.

After my visit to Dr. Israbian on January 5, 2015, he released me completely. The only residual symptoms are chronic bronchitis, or asthmatic bronchitis. He examined me and said the only thing I am allergic to is cold temperatures. I had suspected that because of the pain I had in my bronchial tubes during the first cold snap in the year following my recovery. The doctor said my bronchial tubes were damaged by the illness and the respirator use.

He recommended that we find a warm place to be during the winter months. Again I saw how God had this all planned out when we were in Arizona in March of 2014. The house we bought on Eva Street would be a dwelling place for us sooner than we had thought.

We sold our business in 2015 after a lengthy decision-making process during which I found that being the owner of the business was too stressful for me.

For a job in Arizona, I do taxi work for the Amish people who live there part of the year. I greatly enjoy the interaction with them, as well as the healing I continue to find in the warm climate.

The God who healed me is the same God who wants to be your All in All. He is the One who forgives, heals,

Norman's daughters enjoy Grandpa in
Arizona one year after his brush with death.

redeems, blesses, and satisfies us (Psalm 103:1–5).

I welcome correspondence and invite you to email me at miller5254@gmail.com or write to William E. Miller, 11625 W. 700 S., Millersburg, Indiana 46543.

—Bill Miller

About the Author

Sherilyn (Troyer) Yoder has enjoyed words as long as she can remember. She wrote poetry in first grade, albeit with primitive lines such as, "My teacher is nice. She likes to eat rice." She also wrote numerous creative stories during her elementary years. As she grew older, she became more pragmatic and oddly drawn to grammar and punctuation.

In her early twenties, Sherilyn taught high school classes in grammar and literature, earning the nickname "Miss Grammar." Several years after that, she began editing for several publishing companies. In the bustle of life, rules-oriented editing felt easier than the slow, creative work of writing. Hence, writing fell by the wayside, except for the reams of journals she kept through the years.

When she was asked to help write the story of Bill and Pauline, Sherilyn decided to embark again on the thoughtful work of writing. This is her first book-length published work.

Sherilyn lives in Partridge, Kansas, with her husband

Caleb, a farmer and paramedic, and her son Theodore, who regularly comes up with surprising two-year-old witticisms.

If you would like to contact Sherilyn, you may email her at quillandeasel@gmail.com or write to her in care of Christian Aid Ministries, P.O. Box 360, Berlin, Ohio 44610.

Christian Aid Ministries

Christian Aid Ministries was founded in 1981 as a nonprofit, tax-exempt 501(c)(3) organization. Its primary purpose is to provide a trustworthy and efficient channel for Amish, Mennonite, and other conservative Anabaptist groups and individuals to minister to physical and spiritual needs around the world. This is in response to the command to "…do good unto all men, especially unto them who are of the household of faith" (Galatians 6:10).

Each year, CAM supporters provide approximately 15 million pounds of food, clothing, medicines, seeds, Bibles, Bible story books, and other Christian literature for needy people. Most of the aid goes to orphans and Christian families. Supporters' funds also help to clean up and rebuild for natural disaster victims, put up Gospel billboards in the U.S., support several church-planting efforts, operate two medical clinics, and provide resources for needy families to make their own living. CAM's main purposes for providing aid are to help and encourage God's people and bring the Gospel to a lost and dying world.

CAM has staff, warehouses, and distribution networks in Romania, Moldova, Ukraine, Haiti, Nicaragua, Liberia, Israel, and Kenya. Aside from management, supervisory personnel, and bookkeeping operations, volunteers do most of the work at CAM locations. Each year, volunteers at our warehouses, field bases, Disaster Response Services projects, and other locations donate over 200,000 hours of work.

CAM's ultimate purpose is to glorify God and help enlarge His kingdom. ". . . whatsoever ye do, do all to the glory of God" (1 Corinthians 10:31).

The Way to God
and Peace

We live in a world contaminated by sin. Sin is anything that goes against God's holy standards. When we do not follow the guidelines that God our Creator gave us, we are guilty of sin. Sin separates us from God, the source of life.

Since the time when the first man and woman, Adam and Eve, sinned in the Garden of Eden, sin has been universal. The Bible says that we all have "sinned and come short of the glory of God" (Romans 3:23). It also says that the natural consequence for that sin is eternal death, or punishment in an eternal hell: "Then when lust hath conceived, it bringeth forth sin: and sin, when it is finished, bringeth forth death" (James 1:15).

But we do not have to suffer eternal death in hell. God provided a sacrifice for our sins through the gift of His only Son, Jesus Christ. "For God so loved the world that he gave his only begotten Son, that whosoever believeth in him should not perish, but have everlasting life" (John 3:16).

A sacrifice is something given to benefit someone else.

It costs the giver greatly. Jesus was God's sacrifice. Jesus' death takes away the penalty of sin for all those who accept this sacrifice and truly repent of their sins. To repent of sins means to be truly sorry for and turn away from the things we have done that have violated God's standards (Acts 2:38; 3:19).

Jesus died, but He did not remain dead. After three days, God's Spirit miraculously raised Him to life again. God's Spirit does something similar in us. When we receive Jesus as our sacrifice and repent of our sins, our hearts are changed. We become spiritually alive! We develop new desires and attitudes (2 Corinthians 5:17). We begin to make choices that please God (1 John 3:9). If we do fail and commit sins, we can ask God for forgiveness. "If we confess our sins, he is faithful and just to forgive us our sins, and to cleanse us from all unrighteousness" (1 John 1:9).

Once our hearts have been changed, we want to continue growing spiritually. We will be happy to let Jesus be the Master of our lives and will want to become more like Him. To do this, we must meditate on God's Word and commune with God in prayer. We will testify to others of this change by being baptized and sharing the good news of God's victory over sin and death. Fellowship with a faithful group of believers will strengthen our walk with God (1 John 1:7).